£25.00

3230170167

D0588328

themes for early years

Festivals

Fully revised with CD-ROM

Licence for CD-ROM

IMPORTANT – PERMITTED USE AND WARNINGS – READ CAREFULLY BEFORE INSTALLING

Includes Adobe Reader

Adobe, the Adobe logo, and Reader are either
registered trademarks or trademarks of Adobe
Systems Incorporated in the United States
and/or other countries.

To enable the running of the videos on the
CD-ROM please download the latest version of
Apple QuickTime from http://www.apple.com/
quicktime/download/win.html

**To use the activities on the CD included with this
book, you will need the following:**
● PC with CD and 128 Mb RAM with Microsoft
Windows 98SE or higher
● Mac G3 with CD and 128 Mb RAM with System
9.2 or later (Mac OSX classic model only)
● Facilities for printing and sound
● SVGA screen displaying at least 64K colours at a
screen size of 800 × 600 pixels.

The LITEhouse,
Langside College, Glasgow

themes for early years

Credits

Text © 2006 Carole Court
© 2006 Scholastic Ltd

Published by Scholastic Ltd, Villiers House,
Clarendon Avenue, Leamington Spa,
Warwickshire CV32 5PR

Printed by Bell & Bain Ltd, Glasgow

2 3 4 5 6 7 8 9 0   7 8 9 0 1 2 3 4 5

British Library Cataloguing-in-Publication
Data A catalogue record for this book is
available from the British Library.

ISBN 0-439-96560-8
ISBN 978-0439-96560-6

Visit our website at www.scholastic.co.uk

CD-ROM developed in association with Footmark
Media Ltd.

All songs and rhymes performed by Sally Scott and
Simon Anderson.

Author
Carole Court

Editor
Jane Bishop

Assistant Editor
Niamh O'Carroll

Series Designers
Joy Monkhouse, Anna Oliwa,
Andrea Lewis and Catherine Mason

Designers
Andrea Lewis and Geraldine Reidy

Illustrations
Cathy Hughes

Cover artwork
Maria Maddox

On-screen activities developed in association
with Ugly Studios © 2006, Ugly Studios.

Acknowledgements

Extracts from *Themes for Early Years: Spring & Summer Festivals* by Carole Court (1997, Scholastic Limited):
Sue Cowling for the use of 'The Rakhi' by Sue Cowling © 1997, Sue Cowling. **John Foster** for the use of 'Buddha Day' © 1997, John Foster. **Jean Gilbert** for the use of 'Five Easter Eggs' by Jean Gilbert © 1997, Jean Gilbert. **John Hardwick** for the use of 'On Good Friday' © 1997, John Hardwick. **Penny Kent** for the use of 'The Dragon Boats' and 'Children's Day' by Penny Kent © 1997, Penny Kent. **Tony Mitton** for the use of 'Holi', 'The Egg Song', 'Eid is coming' and 'The Maypole Rhyme' by Tony Mitton © 1997, Tony Mitton. **Barbara Moore** for the use of 'The Story of Baisakhi' and 'A Story for Holi' by Barbara Moore © 1997, Barbara Moore. **Peter Morrell** for the use of 'Holi Time' and 'Five Brave Men' by Peter Morrell © 1997, Peter Morrell. **David Moses** for the use of 'Dragon Boat Race' by David Moses © 1997, David Moses. **Hazel Priestley-Hobbs** for the use of 'Passover' by Hazel Priestley-Hobbs © 1997, Hazel Priestley-Hobbs.
Extracts from *Themes for Early Years: Autumn & Winter Festivals* by Carole Court (1997, Scholastic Limited):
Jackie Andrews for the use of 'The Chinese New Year Story' by Jackie Andrews © 1997, Jackie Andrews. **Clive Barnwell** for the use of 'Ready for Harvest' by Clive Barnwell © 1997, Clive Barnwell. **John Foster** for 'Guru Nanak's Birthday' by John Foster © 1997, John Foster. **Wendy Larmont** for the use of 'Divali Starts Today' by Wendy Larmont © 1997, Wendy Larmont. **Sue Nicholls** for the use of 'Advent Calendar Song' by Sue Nicholls © 1997, Sue Nicholls. **Jan Pollard** for the use of 'Chinese Lion Dance' and 'Carnival for Mardi Gras' by Jan Pollard © 1997, Jan Pollard. **Hazel Priestley-Hobbs** for the use of 'Chinese New Year' by Hazel Priestley-Hobbs © 1997, Hazel Priestley-Hobbs. **Michael Stone** for the use of 'The Story of Divali Festival of Lights' by Susheila Stone © 1997, Susheila Stone.
Sally Scott for the use of 'Janamashtami' and 'Ethiopian New Year' by Sally Scott © 2006, Sally Scott (previously unpublished). **Brenda Williams** for the use of 'The Harvest', 'Palm, Myrtle, Willow', 'This Special Day', 'Long Ago in Egypt', 'Let's Celebrate' and 'Baisakhi Days' by Brenda Williams © 2006, Brenda Williams (previously unpublished).
Qualifications and Curriculum Authority for the use of extracts from QCA/DfEE document Curriculum guidance for the foundation stage © 2000 Qualifications and Curriculum Authority.

Every effort has been made to trace copyright holders and the publishers apologise for any omissions.

Due to the nature of the web, the publisher cannot guarantee the content or links of any of the websites referred to. It is the responsibility of the reader to assess the suitability of websites.

themes for early years

Contents

Autumn and winter

CD-ROM

- All songs sung with musical accompaniment
- All songs music-only version
- All rhymes spoken
- 18 photocopiable pages, including four stories.
- Ten full-colour photographs
- Five on-screen activities
- Three film clips

Introduction

'Festivals' is a topic that can be used throughout the year to celebrate a range of events for a variety of faiths. Exact dates are not always possible as some, such as Easter, depend on the lunar cycle or vary each year. The ways of celebrating can also be regional or individual so memories of a particular festival may differ. The spelling can also vary such as Baisakhi/Vaisakhi or Divali/Diwali/Deepavali.

Many practitioners are reluctant to introduce the topic as they feel unsure about their own level of knowledge, and they are concerned about causing offence in a sensitive area. It is hoped that the information in this book will give you the confidence to undertake the work. Learning about festivals can be extremely enjoyable, and an opportunity for children and adults to find out more, whether there is a child of that faith in the group or not. The children's sections of many libraries often contain relevant books with further information. Always remember that to a person of a particular faith a festival may have a religious significance and should be respected as such.

How to use this book

On page 7 is a Planner which indicates links to the Foundation Stage curriculum. Each activity suggests a suitable Early Learning Goal and Stepping Stone. Try to introduce a new festival through a shared experience such as a story, recount of an experience, discussing a photograph or watching a film clip together.

Many of the festival activities can be used in a cross-curricular way. Apart from being play activities to use across the year, many of them can be incorporated into other themes. For example, Holi, Divali and the Ethiopian New Year all link with a theme such as colour, while Sukkot and Hanukkah link with homes, and Raksha Bandhan with families. Furthermore, many festival stories relate to good triumphing over evil, or illustrate ways to

behave or relate to each other, thereby linking well with many personal and cultural programmes.

In addition to the wide range of activities across the six Areas of Learning there are also suggestions relating to displays (pages 71–74) and, although they relate to four specific displays, these can be adapted to suit any of the festivals in the book too. They are an ideal way to inform families of group activities and can encourage family participation.

What's on the CD-ROM?

New with this series is an accompanying CD-ROM designed to support the learning opportunities in the book. Audio versions of all the songs on pages 75–82 are provided, each with two versions, one full sung version and another with just the musical accompaniment for you to sing your own words to. Spoken versions of the rhymes on pages 83–90 are also included, to provide an opportunity for the children to enjoy listening to them as often as you choose.

All the songs and rhymes are linked to the activities but can also be used on their own. Younger children might find it difficult to join in the complete verse but they will be able to participate in a part or join in a discussion following the reading.

The photocopiable pages in the book are also available to download from the CD-ROM and can be used with variable degrees of adult support. In each case, talk through the activity first and use it as a speaking and listening activity. The stories on these pages are the background to many of the activities. They lend themselves well to drama and other creative activities. There is, however, a need to be sensitive to the religious aspects such as not acting the part of Guru Nanak.

Put the fruit and vegetables on the stall.

Solely on the CD-ROM there are five on-screen activities that relate directly to a festival and an activity idea featured in the book. The way in which these are used will depend on the facilities available and the experience of the children in your group.

Three film clips and ten photographs have also been selected to complement the activities. Many of the ideas will be new experiences for the children and it is hoped that these resources will help them to understand the festivals to a greater extent. Share them with the children and use them for a basis for discussion. Encourage the children to ask questions about what they see and investigate together to find out the answers.

Planner

Use this guide to link the activity ideas into your planning for the six Areas of Learning.

Festivals

Assessment

Assessment, when completed carefully, can help establish a clear understanding of each child's skills, knowledge and progress in all six Areas of Learning. Assessment can also be used to ensure effective coverage of the Stepping Stones and Early Learning Goals.

Use a mixture of different approaches and ensure that the children being assessed are in familiar surroundings and engaged in play and craft activities that they enjoy. Overall, assessments should be ongoing, noted down as soon as possible, or gathered regularly, and always kept up to date. The observations should then be analysed and the need for future support considered. The assessments can then be used to determine future planning.

Opportunities for assessment in this book:

All activities within the book have an Assessment section which provides an indication of what to look out for when observing children perform the task. These suggestions focus on identifying the children's achievements, for example, their participation in discussion, their respect for the beliefs and traditions of others and their willingness to take part. Different procedures will be suitable at different times, depending on the children and the setting; for example:

• Talking, listening and asking questions

This enables practitioners to gain an awareness of what the children know, recall and understand. The process is founded on asking the children open questions, using terms such as, *how*, *why*, *when*, and *where* as this will help to stimulate responses that go beyond a 'yes' or 'no' answer. It is through discussion that it is possible to determine a child's ideas about, and understanding of, faith and belief. These discussions frequently take place during craft or other activities.

• Joining in with play sessions

Joining in with the children's play sessions or role-play situations can provide an extra insight into each child's language, vocabulary and comprehension. Take notes after the session and use these to help support short-term planning, and to provide up-to-date information for other practitioners within your setting, parents and carers. Acting out the stories, joining in with craft activities such as 'Rangoli patterns', page 46, and discussing photographs and film clips all allow the practitioner to gather a wealth of information.

• Collecting samples of achievement

Collect samples of work as well as photographs of a selection of their models and construction. Over time, the materials gathered will constitute an informative and practical record of each child's progress and achievements. Many of the photocopiable activities in the book can be used in this way. The 'Easter story' page 13, 'Light the candles', page 52 and ' Family traditions', page 57 lend themselves well to this form of assessment.

Spring and summer

These ideas will take you from the colourful celebrations for Holi, through Easter, Baisakhi and Pesach to May Day and Raksha Bandhan.

themes for early years

Splatter painting

Art and craft

What you need
Glue; scissors; selection of old magazines; one bright and one darker sheet of background paper per child (approximate size A4); old toothbrushes or similar; bright-coloured paints; aprons; table covering.

What to do
Help the children to cover their clothes and the area, and prepare the paints.

Sing the song 'Holi time' (page 77) together and explain to the children that they are going to do an activity relating to this festival of Holi.

Hand out the magazines and ask the children to each choose and cut out a picture of a person. Show them how to stick their chosen picture in the centre of a piece of dark backing paper. When the glue is dry let them use the toothbrushes to flick some paint over the picture. If they haven't tried 'flicking' paint before you may need to demonstrate the technique. Encourage the use of several colours.

They can then cut out their painting in an irregular shape and mount it onto a sheet of brightly coloured paper.

HOLI
March/April This Hindu festival is celebrated by playing tricks, throwing coloured water over each other, dancing and processions, as a reminder of the playful games of the young Krishna.

Discussion
Explain that the festival of Holi is a time when Hindus remember the games played by the Lord Krishna when he was young. Traditionally, older members of the community are shown great respect but during Holi the young are allowed to play tricks on others. One popular activity is to wear old clothes and throw coloured water on each other.

Follow-up activities
● Read the Holi story on page 91 to the children.
● Draw around a child to make a person shape to splatter with paint.

Differentiation
Demonstrate the technique for younger children. Talk to older children about the effects produced and ways to improve the final piece.

Story sequence

What you need
Copy of 'A story for Holi' on page 91; photocopiable page 11 'Holi story'; scissors; blank pages for the book; hole-punch; loose-leaf ring or ribbon.

Preparation
Copy the photocopiable sheet 'Holi story' to give one per child. Prepare blank pages and a cover page.

What to do
Read the story of Holi to the children. Next show them the photocopiable sheet of pictures that tell the story and talk about each one in turn. Demonstrate how you can cut them out and move them into different orders. Refer to the story and place the pictures in the same sequence.

Give the children their own copies of the sheets and ask them to cut them out very carefully. You may need to help younger children with this. Ask them to place the pictures in the correct order and to retell the story using the pictures as a prompt. As the children talk, record their version of the story onto blank pages. It might be easier to write this in rough first and then copy the draft onto the pages of the book. When complete, punch a hole in the top of all the pages and attach the ring or ribbon.

Discussion
Discuss the content of the pictures. Describe what is happening and why. Talk about the order in which the events took place. Talk about a story having a beginning, middle and end. Find the first and last pages of the book. Can the children remember the order for the middle pages? Explain that the story is important to Hindu families and is about God protecting his followers.

Follow-up activities
- Add extra pages for writing and pictures for a more detailed version of the story.
- Make a class book or display of the story.
- Share other stories of people who were willing to be tested for their faith such as 'Daniel in the lion's den'.

Differentiation
Pre-cut the pictures for younger or less able children and remind them of the story as they sequence. Ask older or more able children to retell the complete story to an audience.

STEPPING STONE
Listen to and join in with stories and poems, one-to-one and also in small groups.

EARLY LEARNING GOAL
Retell narratives in the correct sequence, drawing on language patterns of stories. (CLL)

ASSESSMENT
Observe and record the children's awareness of sequencing in a story.

ON THE CD-ROM
- Photocopiable sheet 'Holi story'
- Photocopiable story 'A story for Holi'

Holi story

● Put the pictures into the same order as the story.

Art and craft

themes for early years

Bonfire display

What you need
Twigs; flame-coloured tissue or crêpe paper; display boards; black backing paper; large sheets of black paper; white paper for speech bubbles; paint; brushes; glue; copy of the poem 'Holi' on page 86.

Preparation
Cover the display board with black paper. Cut out speech bubbles. Prepare the paint area with bright paint and black paper.

What to do
Explain that Hindus frequently celebrate the festival with a communal bonfire. It is a reminder of the Holi story that culminates in a bonfire. Read the rhyme 'Holi' and the description of the bonfire. Explain that the children are going to work together to perform the rhyme and produce their own display.

Support a small group of children in making the bonfire with twigs and paper. Attach this to a piece of black backing paper, which can then be attached to the board. Ask a group of children to paint pictures of the children watching the bonfire. Ask another group to make the adults. When dry, cut them out and add to the display. Read the rhyme to the group. Repeat this on several occasions so that the children gradually learn the words. Show the speech bubbles to the group. Ask the children to quote the first lines of the rhyme while an adult scribes clearly. Continue until the rhyme is completed. Add these to the display.

Discussion
Talk about the ways in which Holi is celebrated. The communal bonfire is just one aspect. It is a reminder of good defeating evil. Just as the children worked together so the adults work together to build the real bonfire. Discuss the safety aspects of visiting a bonfire. Why is it very important to stay a good distance away? What are the dangers and how can the children enjoy a bonfire safely?

> **Follow-up activities**
> ● Use glitter to add stars to the background.
> ● Incorporate the rhyme in a performance.
> ● Dramatise the Holi story, or retell it with puppets.
> ● Visit a Mandir and ask questions about the ways of celebrating Holi.

Differentiation
Vary the amount of support given to learn the rhyme. Ask younger children to concentrate on the quoted lines and involve families in providing support.

STEPPING STONE
Value and contribute to own well-being and self-control.

EARLY LEARNING GOAL
Work as part of a group or class, taking turns and sharing fairly, understanding that there needs to be agreed values and codes of behaviour for groups of people, including adults and children, to work together harmoniously. (PSED)

ASSESSMENT
Observe the way that the children work together and cooperate.

ON THE CD-ROM
● Poem 'Holi'

The Easter story

What you need
A suitable version of the Easter story such as, *The Easter Story* (Ladybird); the song 'Five Easter eggs' on page 80.

Preparation
Arrange the room so that all the children can sit comfortably and have eye contact with the storyteller.

What to do
Begin by explaining that you are going to tell a story that is very special to Christian people. To many people, Easter is just about holidays and chocolate eggs, but in Christian families they remember what happened to Jesus at this time.

Tell the story in an interesting way and allow time for the children to talk about it if they wish. Re-read any sections which the children are not clear about or need reinforcing. Sing the song 'Five Easter eggs' together.

Discussion
Explain that the festival is the most important one in the Christian year and a time when most Christians try to go to church. Some aspects of the story are difficult for children to understand and can be upsetting. The idea of crucifixion can be very disturbing but it was a normal punishment at that time. Jesus explained that it is important for wheat to die as the seed then grows and produces even more wheat. Children can also see that the sun disappears and then rises again and also that plants appear to die in the winter but reappear in the spring. Easter is celebrated all over the world but it is only associated with spring in the northern hemisphere. The many names for it relate to the Jewish festival of Passover such as Påske (Denmark), Pâques (France), Pasen (Holland), Pasqua (Italy), Pascua (Spain), Påsk (Sweden), Pasg (Wales).

EASTER
March/April This important festival in the Christian year marks the joy in the resurrection of Jesus on Easter Day, following the sadness of His crucifixion on Good Friday.

Follow-up activities
- Sing the song 'On Good Friday' on page 79.
- Read the Bible version of the story and listen to a different style of writing.
- Make a timeline of the story.
- Make an Easter card.

Differentiation
Modify the detail of the story according to the children's level of understanding.

STEPPING STONE
Begin to use talk instead of action to rehearse, reorder and reflect on past experience, linking significant events from own experience and from stories, paying attention to sequence and how events lead into one another.

EARLY LEARNING GOAL
Use talk to organise, sequence and clarify thinking, ideas, feelings and events. (CLL)

ASSESSMENT
Record the children's comments during discussion and observe their concentration during the listening part of the activity.

ON THE CD-ROM
- Song 'Five Easter Eggs'
- Song 'On Good Friday'

Mark-making

Easter egg hunt

What you need
The photocopiable sheet 'Find the eggs' on page 15; a set of crayons for each child; a barrier to put between the children such as a large book or folded card; an Easter egg.

Preparation:
Set up the area so that you can see the children's responses but they cannot see either your response, or those of their friends. Ensure that the children can hear your instructions clearly.

What to do:
Work with a small group of children and explain that you are going to prepare an Easter egg hunt. Show the Easter egg to the children and place it under a table or chair and ask individual children to describe where it is. Repeat in a different location. Ask the children to suggest other hiding places and give you the appropriate directions. They can take it turns to give and follow instructions.

Hand out copies of the photocopiable sheet and invite the children to locate the hidden eggs, colouring them in as they do so. Next explain that you are going to hide some more eggs on the paper. Draw an egg on your own sheet, without showing the children, and ask them to listen very carefully and follow your instructions. Describe in detail where you have drawn the egg, and encourage the children to try and draw one in the same location on their own sheets. Encourage them to ask questions if that helps them. These children can then play with other adults or children, taking turns as instructors.

Discussion
Talk about good hiding places for the eggs. Discuss the appropriate vocabulary and encourage children to ask questions such as: *Is it behind the big flower or the little one?* Explain that this idea is based on a traditional activity when the 'Easter Bunny' is believed to leave Easter eggs hidden in gardens.

Follow-up
● Organise an Easter egg hunt for the children and their families.
● Make decorations and cards based on the Easter egg theme.
● Make an Easter egg tree.

Differentiation
Discuss the picture prior to the activity with children who require additional support. Use the relevant positional language to locate possible hiding places for the Easter eggs. Limit the vocabulary used. For children requiring a challenge, encourage the asking of questions and a wider range of vocabulary.

STEPPING STONE
Respond to simple instructions.

EARLY LEARNING GOAL
Sustain attentive listening, responding to what they have heard by relevant comments, questions and actions. (CLL)

ASSESSMENT
Observe the confidence with which children locate the Easter eggs. Record the vocabulary used by the children and the areas where further development is needed.

ON THE CD-ROM
● Photocopiable sheet 'Find the eggs'

Find the eggs

● Can you find the eggs hidden in the picture?

Outdoor
environment

Easter games

What you need
Instrument (drum or tambourine); hard-boiled egg for each child; spoons; safe outside area.

Preparation
Take the children outdoors for some warm-up activities. Tap the drum or tambourine and ask them to walk around the space without touching anyone else, following the sound of the instrument. Vary the activity by asking them to go quickly or slowly. Practise stop and go signals.

What to do
Divide the children into five mixed-ablility groups with an adult who will accompany them. Indicate the start and finish times of each activity by the sound of the instrument. Some activities will need to be repeated.
- Egg and spoon race: children carry their egg on a spoon to a given point and return to their team, without touching the egg.
- Egg rolling race: children race to a given point rolling the eggs in front of them. The egg must reach the point – not the child!
- Throwing and catching: children throw their eggs into the air and catch them. If they drop the egg they are 'out'.
- Throw the egg: see how far the children can throw their eggs.
- Egg hunt: hand out copies of the photocopiable sheet on page 15 and invite the children to find the hidden Easter eggs.

Finish with a stretching exercise using the drum/tambourine to give instructions for different parts of the body to stretch out and then return to the shell. Eventually the children use their whole bodies to jump up and stretch. Sit together and sing the song 'Five Easter eggs', on page 80, together.

Discussion
The idea of playing games with eggs originated in pagan spring festivals and rituals. They are now the basis for Easter games in many countries such as throwing and catching in France and egg-rolling in northern Britain, Germany, Switzerland and America where children traditionally roll their eggs on the White House lawn. Egg shackling is popular in some areas and involves hitting two eggs together to see which is the hardest.

Follow-up activities
- Find out about local customs such as bottle kicking, ducking and ball games, which are played on Easter Monday.
- Look at the designs on some Eastern European decorated eggs. Decorate hard-boiled eggs or draw and decorate some on paper.

Differentiation
Choose activities to meet the needs of the children. Vary the distances according to the age and size of the children.

STEPPING STONE
Move body position as necessary.

EARLY LEARNING GOAL
Show awareness of space, of themselves and of others. (PD)

ASSESSMENT
Observe the children's physical movements and awareness of space.

ON THE CD-ROM
- Song 'Five Easter eggs'

Outdoor environment

themes for early years

STEPPING STONE

Show an interest in why things happen and how things work.

EARLY LEARNING GOAL

Ask questions about why things happen and how things work. (KUW)

ASSESSMENT

Observe the children's participation in the discussion and interest shown as the plants grow.

New life

What you need
Cress seeds; flower seeds which germinate quickly; hyacinth bulb; indoor and outdoor flowering bulbs; blotting paper; tray; seed tray; compost; bulb pot; fibre; bulb jar; water; outdoor space.

What to do
Explain to the children that, dividing into two groups, they are either going to watch some seeds or bulbs being planted. Tell them that they will only watch one of these so they will need to watch and listen very carefully and then tell the other group what happened. Divide the children into two groups, one for seed planting, and one for bulbs.

Encourage them to ask questions as they watch.
- **Seeds**: Dampen the blotting paper and sprinkle the cress seeds on top. Do not allow the paper to dry out. For the second seed planting, fill the seed tray with compost. Follow the directions on the packet to sow the seeds in drills. Cover and moisten the compost.
- **Bulbs**: Fill the bulb jar with water as far as the 'neck'. Place the hyacinth bulb on top so that the roots will be able to grow down into the water. Now, use the bulb fibre to plant some indoor bulbs in a pot at an appropriate depth. Moisten the fibre.

Place all four containers in a place where they can receive light and warmth. Water them when needed and observe what happens.

Plant the outdoor seeds and bulbs with the other group.

Let the children keep a record of what they see, either by writing down some words or by drawing what they can see happening. Keep the children's observations and predictions for future use.

Invite children from each of the groups to describe how the bulbs/ seeds were planted to the children in the other group.

Discussion
Talk about the needs of the plants. Why were they placed in a light, warm position? What will happen if they dry out? Which do they think will grow the quickest? Discuss the other aspects of new life that can be seen near Easter time such as tadpoles growing, and lambs being born. Read the rhyme 'The egg song', on page 89, together. The word 'Easter' is derived from 'Eostre' the goddess of spring, and in the northern hemisphere this is the time of year when Easter is celebrated. Easter, spring and eggs are all associated with new growth and new life.

> ### Follow-up activities
> - Make observational drawings to record growth, and display these near the indoor growing plants.
> - Plant individual yoghurt pots with seeds for the children to take home.
> - Act out the growth of a tadpole, plant or bird.

ON THE CD-ROM
- Poem 'The egg song'

Differentiation
Involve the younger or less able children with more of the ground preparation and encourage older children to lead the discussion.

themes for early years

Five brave men

BAISAKHI
13 April Important Sikh festival marking the time when baptised Sikhs began to wear the five Ks.

STEPPING STONE
Gain an awareness of the cultures and beliefs of others.

EARLY LEARNING GOAL
Begin to know about their own cultures and beliefs and those of other people. (KUW)

ASSESSMENT
Observe the children to judge their understanding of the parts played by the main characters.

What you need
'The story of Baisakhi' (page 92–93); the song 'Five brave men' on page 78; paints (including skin-coloured paint); brushes; paper; black felt-tipped pen; backing paper; glue; material; scissors.

Preparation
Draw large speech bubbles for each child, mount the background display paper, and prepare the area to be used for painting by covering the surfaces, mixing the paints and cutting the paper.

What to do
Use the photocopiable sheet to tell the children the story of the five men who were willing to give up their lives for their faith.

Recap the story and then ask the children to paint the main characters. These might include the crowd, the Guru, the first volunteer, the other four volunteers, the men in their new robes. Let the children choose which to paint and which colours they would like to use.

While the paintings are drying sing the song 'Five brave men' together. Cut out the dry paintings, mount them onto backing paper and add speech bubbles. Ask the children to suggest a quote from each of the characters and record it for them in the bubbles. Add a title for your display.

Discussion
Explain that the first Baisakhi happened when Sikhs were being persecuted. Guru Gobind Singh wanted to test people's faith and asked them to commit themselves to Sikhism. From this time baptised Sikhs wore the five Ks (Kachera, Kara, Kesh, Khanga and Kirpan) as symbols of their faith. The Guru believed that God loved everyone equally and asked Sikhs to take just one name – Singh (lion) for men and Kaur (princess) for women. Talk about the feelings of the people involved, who were worried about what they were asked to do and relieved when the men were still alive. Talk about other people who are brave. There might be a news story about a heroic rescue that you can discuss. Discuss the role of a leader. Who do the children respect as leaders?

Follow-up activities
- Listen to stories about brave people such as Grace Darling.
- Talk about the symbols associated with different organisations such as the uniform worn in school, for Beavers and Rainbows or by a worker in the supermarket.

ON THE CD-ROM
- Photocopiable story 'The story of Baisakhi'
- Photograph showing Khanga and Kara
- Song 'Five brave men'

Differentiation
Talk to younger or less able children as they paint and encourage them to include detail. Support older or more able children in writing their own comments in the speech bubbles.

themes for early years

Belonging

What you need
A collection of 'symbols of belonging' such as a football club scarf, a school badge, Brownie uniform, a cross; the five Ks or pictures of them; table and wall space for a display; paper; scissors; sticky tape; the rhyme 'Baisakhi days' on page 90.

Preparation
Bring together the materials to start a group collection, put up a group notice to inform families of the collection and invite them to make contributions. Explain that, for security reasons, you would prefer not to have valuable items. Prepare the display area and write a large title such as 'Belonging'. Borrow religious artefacts from families, schools or LEA resource centres.

What to do
Ask the children to sit so that they can all see the artefacts. Show them the non-religious ones first and discuss what they represent. Give the children the opportunity to hold the object. Follow this with examining the religious artefacts in a similar way but emphasise that they must be treated with great respect. Concentrate on the five Ks and explain their significance to Sikhs and to Baisakhi.

Read the rhyme 'Baisakhi days' with together. Encourage the children to add to the display over time.

STEPPING STONE
Have a sense of self as a member of different communities.

EARLY LEARNING GOAL
Have a developing respect for their own cultures and beliefs and those of other people. (PSED)

ASSESSMENT
Observe the ways in which children treat religious artefacts with respect. Do they treat both familiar and unfamiliar objects with equal respect?

The Khanga is the comb.

The Kachera is white cotton underwear similar to shorts.

The Kara is worn on the right wrist.

The Kirpan is a small curved sword which is only to be used in defence.

The Kesh or long hair is a symbol of faith.

Discussion
Discuss why symbols are used and how they make people feel that they belong. What badges or symbols do the children have? Are there any special ones that they collect? Explain how the five Ks are important to Sikhs and how Guru Gobind Singh asked them to wear them as a symbol of their commitment to their faith.

Follow-up activities
● Continually add to the collection.
● Discuss a symbol for your group to represent their interests. Ask the children to suggest possible items to be included such as a book, paintbrush, computer, or ball.
● Design a flag using the group's symbols.

ON THE CD-ROM
● Photograph of Khanga and Kara
● Poem 'Baisakhi days'

Differentiation
Limit the symbols for younger or less able children. Widen the range for older or more able children, and introduce some that are unfamiliar.

Maths

themes for early years

STEPPING STONE
Use mathematical
language in play.

EARLY LEARNING GOAL
Recognise numerals 1 to
9. (MD)

ASSESSMENT
In addition to assessing
the mathematical areas,
observation of physical
development can take
place.

Magic five

What you need
Items as required by the ideas below.

Preparation
Set out the activities around the room.

What to do
Ask the children to sit on the floor and explain to them that all these
activities have a connection with the number five. Start by counting
five fingers together, do this slowly so that the children are actually
counting fingers and not just reciting the numerals. Ask them to join
in some number action rhymes such as 'Five currant buns', 'Five little
ducks' or 'Five little peas'.

Let the children choose from these ideas:
- paint or draw the numeral;
- draw a hand and number the fingers;
- score five goals;
- skip five times;
- knock down five skittles;
- use a number line up to five;
- play Kim's game with five objects;
- draw or paint five objects;
- make patterns with five pegs in a board;
- thread five beads;
- find the odd-one-out where one set is not five;
- cut and stick five pictures;
- decorate the numeral five;
- make a number five using play dough;
- decorate biscuits with patterns of five currants or cherries;
- sort a collection of objects into sets of five;
- make patterns with polygons.

When the children have tried a selection of activities bring them back
together and ask them to take turns in telling the group what they did
with the number five.

Discussion
Talk about the importance of five in Sikhism. The Punjabi word for five
is panj and the area is known as the Punjab, which means five rivers.
In addition, at Baisakhi there were five volunteers and followers were
asked to wear five symbols of their faith, the five Ks. Are there any
numbers that are especially important to the children? (Perhaps their
own age or the number of their house.)

Follow-up activities
- Ask the children to stay quiet for five seconds. Can any of them
  stay quiet for five minutes?
- Count in fives.
- Play 'Buzz' counting to 20 but replacing every fifth number with
  'buzz'; *1 2 3 4 buzz 6 7 8 9 buzz 11 12 13 14 buzz.*
- Use the photocopiable sheet 'Sets of five' on page 21 to reinforce
  counting skills to five.

Differentiation
Allocate tasks according to the ability of the children.

ON THE CD-ROM
- Photocopiable sheet 'Sets of five'
- Song 'Five brave men'

Sets of five

● Add some objects to make sets of five.

Food

Let's cook

STEPPING STONE
Have a positive approach to new experiences.

EARLY LEARNING GOAL
Continue to be interested, excited and motivated to learn. (PSED)

ASSESSMENT
Observe the accuracy with which children weigh the ingredients and the attempts to follow illustrated instructions. Use the individual pictures on page 23 as a sequencing assessment activity. Observe the enthusiasm shown by the children.

What you need
Scales; rolling pins; boards; table covering; cookery aprons; washing-up facilities; cooker; pan; ingredients as listed on page 23; mixing bowl; jam (optional); washing facilities; photocopiable page 23 'Making chapattis'.

Preparation
Prepare a clean and hygienic area, collect together the ingredients and utensils, enlarge the photocopiable sheet 'Making chapattis' and provide copies for the children. Help the children to wash their hands, put on aprons, roll up or cover sleeves, and tie back hair.

What to do
Explain that Baisakhi is a time when Sikhs like to visit the Gurdwara. Each Gurdwara has a langar or kitchen where meals are prepared and shared with all visitors – whether Sikh or not. The children are going to be involved in the making of chappati, which is a popular Indian food. They will not be able to do the actual cooking for safety reasons but they will be able to enjoy the final product.

Show the group the enlarged instructions and talk through the process using the appropriate language of instruction at each stage. Follow the instructions according to the recipe. Share and enjoy the chappati – perhaps with a little jam. Involve all the children in washing up if this is practical.

Discussion
Discuss the langar and the willingness to share food. Sikhs believe in equality and their kitchen is open to all. Do the children feel that this is a good way to be? Talk about the change in the ingredients both before and after cooking. Ask them to describe the food through the different stages. Does the process remind them of any other recipes? Do they eat similar foods at home?

Discuss the need for cleanliness. Explain why it is so important for the table and their hands to be clean. Explain the safety reasons for not cooking themselves.

Follow-up activities
● Arrange a visit to a Gurdwara.
● Taste other Indian foods.
● Take photographs of the different cooking stages and use to sequence, prompt recording and display. (Remember to obtain parental consent before taking photographs of the children.)

Differentiation
Encourage more experienced children to follow the instructions. Show them how to look at the illustrations, discuss and do. Younger or less able children may need to have support when weighing.

ON THE CD-ROM
● Photocopiable sheet 'Making chapattis'

Making chappatis

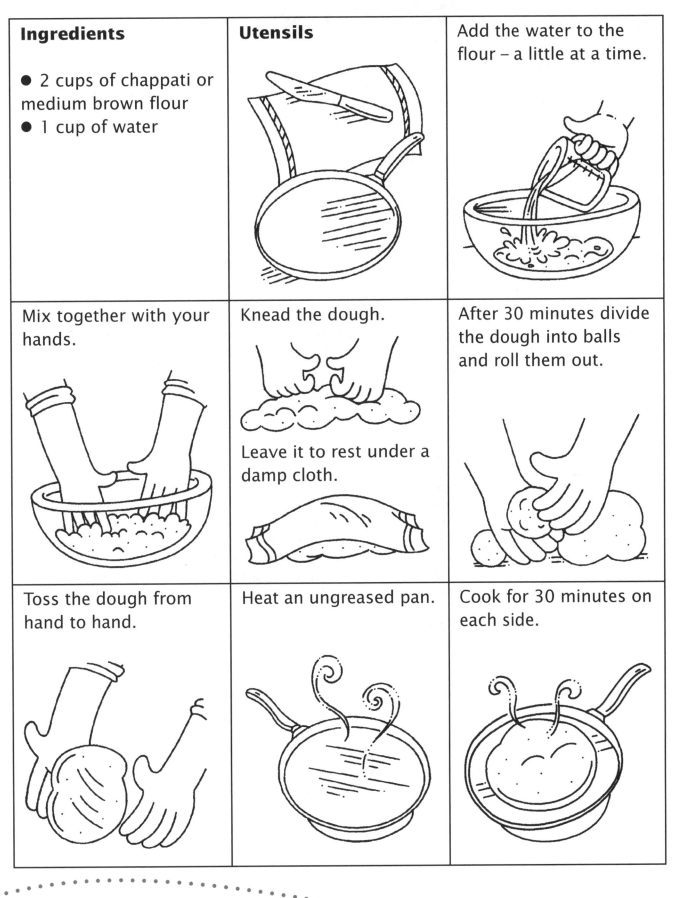

Ingredients

- 2 cups of chappati or medium brown flour
- 1 cup of water

Utensils

Add the water to the flour – a little at a time.

Mix together with your hands.

Knead the dough.

Leave it to rest under a damp cloth.

After 30 minutes divide the dough into balls and roll them out.

Toss the dough from hand to hand.

Heat an ungreased pan.

Cook for 30 minutes on each side.

Sound

themes for early years

STEPPING STONE
Demonstrate the control necessary to hold a shape or fixed position.

EARLY LEARNING GOAL
Move with control and coordination. (PD)

ASSESSMENT
Observe the children's movement and interpretation of music.

Bhangra dancing

What you need
An example of bhangra music; internet access to find examples/sources of bhangra music, and images/film clips of bhangra dancing; CD player; space to move to the music; a drum; bells (craft shops or educational suppliers) narrow elastic.

Preparation
Make ankle bells by attaching a bell (or several) to a loose-fitting circle of narrow elastic. Prepare the area and set up the equipment ready for the children to listen to the music.

What to do
Ask the children to sit on the floor with a small space around them. Show them the internet clips/images and discuss the dancing. Put on the CD and listen to the music, tapping the rhythm on the drum. Ask the children to form a circle and join you in tapping out the rhythm on their hands. Now can they stand up and keep the beat with their foot?

Distribute the ankle bells and repeat the foot tapping. When the children are confident in this, ask them to try to hop at the same time. Encourage them to make different shapes and movements while keeping up the rhythm. Ask individual children to enter the circle and dance if they feel confident to do this. Gradually reduce the volume until the children sit down to finish. Look at the images again and relate them to their own experience.

Discussion
Explain that Baisakhi is a festival that takes place chiefly in the Punjab area of India. This is a farming area, and the festival takes place at the time of harvest. Many of the movements in the traditional dance represent the actions of the farming year. Costumes are usually loose and bright and can be extremely elaborate. It is a dance that requires great stamina. The drum is vital as the dancers follow its beat.

Follow-up activities
- Look at pictures of the traditional costumes of bhangra dancing. These can be found in many books about India or traditional folk dancing.
- Think about the movements involved in farming and try to develop actions that represent them such as sowing seeds or reaping.

Differentiation
Ask younger children to move freely to the music. Encourage older or more able children to develop actions relating to harvest.

Bitter and sweet

STEPPING STONE
Examine objects and living things to find out more about them.

EARLY LEARNING GOAL
Investigate objects and materials by using all of their senses as appropriate. (KUW)

ASSESSMENT
Record the children's estimates and note their accuracy.

What you need
A variety of sweet and bitter foods such as: lemon, plain cooking chocolate, vinegar, sweet chocolate, sugar, sweet and sour apples (try to include some foods that are likely to be new to the group); large and small sheets of paper; drawing materials; knives; teaspoons; sticky tape; scissors; photograph of a Seder plate.

PESACH
Spring (Date varies) This Jewish festival (Passover) celebrates the time when Moses led the Israelites out of slavery in Egypt and towards the 'Promised Land'. The celebratory meal and associated activities are reminders of that time.

Preparation
Cut four large circles of paper and label two of them 'Sweet' and the other two 'Bitter'. Make it easier for the children to identify them by making the paper or the writing in different colours.

What to do
Look together at the photograph of the Seder plate on the CD-ROM and talk about the different foods. Show the children the selection of food you have and ask them to draw what they can see. Ensure you end up with at least two illustrations of each food. Cut these out and label them with the name of the food.

Ask the children to guess if the foods are bitter or sweet and to stick one of the illustrations into the appropriate circle. Next, give the children small samples of the foods to taste and ask them to decide again whether they are bitter or sweet. They should then stick the second set of illustrations onto the second set of large circles. Compare the two versions to see how accurate the children's first estimates had been.

Discussion
Explain that sweet and bitter foods are associated with Pesach as a reminder of the story of the Jews being led from slavery by Moses. Jewish people remember the bitterness of slavery and the sweetness of freedom. Sing the song 'Passover', on page 75, together. Show the children the photograph of the Seder plate and talk about some of the foods associated with the meal such as the charoset (a reminder of the mortar used when Jews were slaves), parsley (a symbol of springtime) or matzos (to remind them of leaving Egypt in a great hurry).

Follow-up activities
● Carry out a survey of favourite foods. Are any of them bitter?
● Play tasting games, trying familiar foods when blindfolded.
● Make and taste charoset.

ON THE CD-ROM
● Photograph of a Seder plate
● Song 'Passover'

Differentiation
Provide less able children with pictures of the foods to sort. Encourage older or more able children to take a greater part in discussions.

themes for early years

Storytelling

What you need
Notebook; pen; small beanbag or similar object; card; paper; drawing materials; stapler; sticky tape.

Preparation
Clear a space so that all the children can sit in a circle together.

What to do
Ask the children to sit down and explain that you are all going to tell a story together. Choose one that is familiar to them such as a traditional story or one that has been read recently. Hold the beanbag as you give the introduction to the story. Pass the beanbag to another child who continues it. The beanbag is gradually passed around the group until the story is complete.

Once the children are confident in listening to each other, continuing the story, and only talking when they have the beanbag, start a story that is new to the children. Introduce some characters and encourage the children to make up their own imaginary story. As an example you could start with, *Once upon a time there was a girl who lived with her aunt in the middle of... One day, when they were digging in their garden they found...*

Record the completed story and retell it to them. When they are happy with the final version, make it into a book and ask the children to illustrate it. Put the finished book into your book corner to be read whenever the children choose.

Discussion
Explain that, during the special Pesach meal, a traditional story is told and children play a vital part. They ask the initial questions which begin the story. Children might follow the story in their own illustrated version of the Hagadah. Talk about the use of the beanbag. Explain the importance of listening and only talking when it is your turn. Encourage them to think of what might happen next and predict what a character might do.

STEPPING STONE
Listen to favourite nursery rhymes, stories and songs. Join in with repeated refrains, anticipating key events and important phrases.

EARLY LEARNING GOAL
Sustain attentive listening, responding to what they have heard by relevant comments, questions or actions. (CLL)

ASSESSMENT
Observe the children's listening skills.

Follow-up activities
● Make the book in a shape appropriate to the story. Add 'lift-up pages' or 'opening doors' with the children's illustrations underneath.
● Look at examples of Hebrew writing as would be used in the Hagadah.
● Make the story into a sequencing activity or draw pictures for a wall display.
● Practise skills of sequencing and prediction by using the photocopiable sheet 'What happens next?' on page 27.

Differentiation
Begin with very short stories for the youngest children. Work with the older children to produce their own original story.

ON THE CD-ROM
● Photocopiable sheet 'What happens next?'

What happens next?

● Look at the pictures and draw what happens next.

themes for early years

Leaving home

What you need
Paper; drawing materials; sticky tape or staples; card; copy of the rhyme 'Long ago in Egypt' on page 83.

Preparation
Prepare a simple bag for the demonstration, cut out five or ten small cards out or each child.

What to do
Explain that the festival of Pesach is a reminder of a time when Jewish people were forced to leave their homes in a big hurry. They were only able to take absolute essentials with them. Read the rhyme 'Long ago in Egypt' with the children.

Ask the children what they would choose to take with them? Dramatise the experience of packing and leaving home in a hurry. Ask the group to consider a number of precious items and list their suggestions. Are there any common choices? Ask the children to make a bag to hold reminders of their special possessions. Demonstrate making a simple paper bag decorated with drawings of people and places that are important to them. Help them to fix the sides with sticky tape or staples. Distribute the small cards and ask the children to draw a special belonging on each one. Remind them of their original list but give them the opportunity to change their minds if they wish. Place these in the bag so that they children can pretend to be ready to leave.

Discussion
Talk about the people and places that are important to individual children. How do they choose? Do they remember happy times spent together or people who have been kind to them. Were the possessions associated with particular people or activities? Is it useful or just for fun? How do children think that it feels to have to leave home in a hurry? Would they be scared or excited? Be aware that there could be some children in the group who have already had this experience.

Follow-up activities
- Talk about occasions when children can remember feeling scared, happy, sad or excited. How did they react? Who supported them and shared the experience?
- Dramatise a family preparing to leave in a hurry.

Differentiation
Encourage children to extend their understanding of the feelings of others. Younger children will need support to understand how it might feel.

ON THE CD-ROM
- Poem 'Long ago in Egypt

Food

themes for early years

Purim

What you need
Access to an oven; mixing bowl; baking tray; rolling pins; round cutters; teaspoons; cooling rack; bowls or plates; 50g sugar; 50g margarine; 75g plain flour; 25g ground almonds or finely chopped nuts (check with parents for any nut allergies); one teaspoon cinnamon; aprons; cleaning materials.

Preparation
Ask the children to wash their hands, push up their sleeves and wear aprons, prepare the ingredients and utensils, set the oven at 180ºC or Gas mark 4.

What to do
Together with the children, weigh out all the ingredients and lightly flour the baking tray. Involve the children in beating the margarine and sugar together. Gradually add the flour and nuts before kneading the mixture well. Divide the mixture so that the children can roll it and use the cutters to cut into circles. Fold and pinch the biscuits to form the shape of a three-cornered hat. Space them on the baking tray and sprinkle cinnamon in the centres. Bake for 15–20 minutes and cool on a wire rack.

While the biscuits are cooking ask all of the children to help with the clearing up. The children can take their biscuits home or eat them together at snack time.

Discussion
Explain that the biscuits are made for the Jewish festival of Purim. Haman was the Prime Minister and he became very angry because Mordecai, a Jewish leader, refused to bow down to him. Haman persuaded the king that all of the Jews should be killed. However, Mordecai's niece, Esther, was the queen and she persuaded the king that she too would have to die. He reversed the order, Haman was killed and Mordecai became Prime Minister. The festival is celebrated by Jewish people visiting the synagogue and every time Haman's name is mentioned in the story the people shout, stamp and use noise-makers.

SPECIAL DAYS: PURIM
Jewish spring festival which takes place four weeks before Pesach. It celebrates the saving of the Jews of Persia. In the synagogue, as the story is read, the people make noise so that the name of Haman cannot be heard.

Follow-up activities
- Make paper-plate puppets to act the story.
- Make a noise-maker by folding a paper plate and stapling the edge. Fill it with rice or dried peas and decorate to form Haman's face; make it as miserable as possible. Attach a stick to make it easier to rattle.
- Tell the story of Esther and Haman. Every time Haman's name is said, the children should make noise so that it cannot be heard.

Differentiation
Vary the discussion according to the children's understanding. Ask more searching questions for the more thoughtful children.

themes for early years

May Day

What you need
Paper; empty scrapbook; glue; scissors; access to a photocopier; notebook; examples of the type of materials that you want to collect; photograph on the CD-ROM of children dancing around a maypole.

Preparation
Make a poster asking families for assistance in compiling a collection of memories of May Day. Display, and copy the notes to send home with the children.

What to do
Tell the children that you are trying to find out about memories that anyone in their families might have of May Days in their childhood. Show them the photograph of the children dancing around the maypole on the CD-ROM and explain that you want to borrow old photographs or newspaper articles which can be copied to make a scrapbook. Show the contributions to the children as they come in, valuing each one however small. Arrange these in the scrapbook very carefully.

Double-mount some of the items and add bright and interesting captions. If contributions are hand-written, consider adding a typed version for children who can read it for themselves. Share the book with the children and encourage them to share it with their families, perhaps when they come to collect or deliver the children.

Invite one or two members of the community to visit the group to share their own memories first hand. Record their contributions and copy the main points into the scrapbook. Encourage the children to listen and to ask questions.

Discussion
Explain to the children that May Day is thought to have developed from the Roman festival of Maia. Dancing around the maypole probably originated in medieval times and then, in the nineteenth century, it became associated with Labour Day when workers took part in processions. Talk about local customs and discuss whether they are still carried out today.

STEPPING STONE
Begin to differentiate between past and present.

EARLY LEARNING GOAL
Find out about past and present events in their own lives, and in those of their families and other people they know. (KUW)

ASSESSMENT
Record the questions asked by the children.

SPECIAL DAYS: MAY DAY
1 May Traditions have Roman, medieval and Celtic connections, associated with the ancient goddess of flowers, Flora. Customs include flowers, processions, Maypole dancing and a May Queen.

Follow-up activities
- Make floral decorations such as a crown decorated with white flowers, hair and dress decorations, floral hoops and garlands.
- Try a simple country dance involving moving in a circle, clapping and skipping; wearing bells on the ankles.
- See the display 'May Day' on page 73.
- Read the poem 'The Maypole rhyme' (page 84) with the children.

Differentiation
Rehearse questions with younger children. Ask more confident children to learn the chorus of the rhyme to perform to the guests.

ON THE CD-ROM
- Photograph of a maypole dance
- Poem 'The Maypole rhyme'

Art and craft

Children's Day

What you need
A bunch of irises and leaves in a vase; variety of drawing and/or painting materials; a copy of Van Gogh's painting *Irises*; copy of the rhyme 'Children's Day' on page 89.

> **SPECIAL DAYS: CHILDREN'S DAY**
> **5 May** Japanese festival formerly known as Boy's Day.

STEPPING STONE
Begin to use representation as a means of communication.

EARLY LEARNING GOAL
Respond in a variety of ways to what they see, hear, smell, touch and feel. (CD)

ASSESSMENT
Examine the children's completed work and evaluate them with the whole group.

Preparation
Arrange the room so that all of the children can see the vase of flowers clearly and have an area to draw or paint (they can be at various heights and angles so that different views can be obtained). Place the materials within easy reach of the children.

What to do
Ask the children to choose the materials that they would like to use and to sit so that they have a clear view of the flowers. Look together at the painting by Van Gogh and compare it with the flowers in the vase. Encourage them to examine the flowers closely and then to make their own paintings, trying to copy the flowers as accurately as possible. Point out the shapes of the flowers and leaves and the bright colours they can see. Some children might find it easier concentrating on copying a single flower rather than a whole display.

Discussion
Read the rhyme 'Children's Day' about celebrating the day and explain that the festival is Japanese and was originally just for boys. Its activities and symbolism emphasise the qualities of strength and determination that are thought to be desirable in children. What do the children think about this? What other qualities do they like to see; perhaps caring and tenderness? One of the reasons that the iris is associated with the festival is that the leaves are thought to resemble the blades of the samurai warriors' swords. Another symbol is the carp, a really strong fish which is difficult to catch, representing power and determination. Healthy food is eaten at the festival to continue this theme. Celebrations take place each year on 5 May.

> ### Follow-up activities
> ● Make carp kites on poles with a wired open mouth and tissue paper body.
> ● Have a healthy eating day.
> ● Use the iris leaves for splatter printing or to make rubbings.
> ● See the display 'Children's Day' on page 74.

Differentiation
Limit the number of flowers used for younger or less able children.

ON THE CD-ROM
● Poem 'Children's Day'

Sound

themes for early years

Wesak

STEPPING STONE
Begin to accept the needs of others, with support.

EARLY LEARNING GOAL
Consider the consequences of their words and actions for themselves and others. (PSED)

ASSESSMENT
Observe evidence of the children's understanding of actions having consequences.

What you need
Facilities to play some quiet reflective music; copy of the rhyme 'Buddha Day' on page 86.

Preparation
Clear an area large enough for the children to sit comfortably and without touching each other.

What to do
At the end of a busy session ask the children to sit very quietly and still. They may like to close their eyes. Play some restful music. While they are listening, ask them to think about the session and all of the things that they have done. Reflect on the actions and words and think about the consequences. Have they been kind to each other and shared the toys? Have they helped someone who needed them? Did they think of other children as well as themselves? Start with the negative and move to the positive so that children leave with positive feelings about themselves.

SPECIAL DAYS: WESAK
May/June. In the Theravada Buddhist tradition, Wesak marks the birth, death and enlightenment of the Buddha, celebrated with the decoration of homes and temples with flowers, candles, lanterns and incense.

Discussion
Talk about the consequences of our actions and the effect that what we say and do has on other people. How could they have changed what they did or said? What were the good things that they did? Did they make anyone smile? How can they try to increase the positive aspect tomorrow?

Many Buddhists undertake a similar activity at the end of the day when they evaluate their actions and their consequences. The Buddha's teachings included: greed and selfishness hurt us; don't be self-centred; respect others; be kind; all life is important; don't steal or lie; don't hurt anyone. Talk about ways that these ideals can be applied to daily life such as being kind to animals or giving to charity. To Theravada Buddhists the festival of Wesak marks the birth, death and enlightenment of the Buddha. It is marked by placing flowers, candles and incense sticks before images as a mark of respect. Light plays a prominent part with bodhi trees being decorated with lights and lanterns. Read and discuss the rhyme 'Buddha Day'.

Follow-up activities
- End your session with this activity regularly (once a week). Find opportunities during each session to listen to children properly and to allow them time for reflection.
- Listen to stories of the Buddha.
- Try to find opportunities to make other people smile.
- Make decorations such as garlands, lanterns cards and flowers.

ON THE CD-ROM
- Poem 'Buddha day'

Differentiation
Remind younger children about some of their actions. Help older children to relate the activity to the Buddhist way of life.

Water

Dragon Boat Festival

STEPPING STONE
Show curiosity and interest by facial expression, movement or sound.

EARLY LEARNING GOAL
Investigate objects and materials by using all of their senses as appropriate. (KUW)

ASSESSMENT
Note the questions asked by the children and the curiosity they show.

What you need
Aprons; large water tray; wide variety of objects to test for floating and sinking; two trays; labels.

Preparation
Prepare the area for water play, collect the materials, label the trays 'floats' and 'sinks', ask the children to wear aprons.

What to do
Allow the children some free play in the water tray. This will give them the opportunity to experiment with the objects and to observe whether they sink or float.

Once they have all had the chance to try some items out, work as a group and take each item in turn to test if it floats or sinks. Ask the children to predict what will happen each time and then test their ideas.

They can use what they found out in free play, and previous experiences when playing, to determine what they think will happen. Finally, sort the objects onto the appropriate labelled trays to indicate 'floats' or 'sinks'.

Discussion
Talk about the observations and predictions as they occur. Remind the children of earlier observations and results and encourage them to transfer this to the new object.

Explain that during the Chinese Dragon Boat festival boat races are held. They relate to the story of Qu Yuan who was a patriot, leader and poet. He felt that the people should join with neighbouring areas to defeat the Kingdom of Chuan. The King refused to follow his advice and sent him away. When he was proved right Qu Yuan tried to kill himself by jumping into the Mik Law River. The people tried to save him but were unable to and his body was never recovered. To protect him from the predators in the river they threw in bamboo tubes filled with rice, in the hope that these would be eaten instead. The bamboo is now replaced by jung gi (savoury or sweet rice dishes wrapped in bamboo leaves). The races are a reminder of the race to try to save him. The boats are decorated in bright colours and with dragon heads to frighten the fish.

SPECIAL DAYS: DRAGON BOAT FESTIVAL
June Annual dragon boat races take place as a reminder of a popular leader who drowned himself. In an attempt to ward off predators, followers raced into the river and threw in parcels of rice.

Follow-up activities
● Sing the song 'Dragon boat race' on page 76 and join in with rowing actions.
● Make a model dragon boat and decorate it with a colourful head.

Differentiation
With younger children support their play in the water tray and help them explore the objects thoroughly. Let older children work independently.

ON THE CD-ROM
● Poem 'The dragon boats'
● Song 'Dragon Boat race'

themes for early years

Raksha Bandhan

What you need
Sheets of foil; small paper doilies; scissors; stapler; glue; scraps of shiny material; paper; pencils; a rakhi wrist decoration or a picture of one; copy of the rhyme 'The Rakhi' on page 87.

Preparation
Cut circles of foil either 4cm larger or slightly smaller than the doilies.

What to do
Read the rhyme 'The Rakhi' and explain its significance. Show the children a rakhi wrist decoration and point out the main features such as the shape, different layers and decoration. Ask them to design their own rakhi using the materials available.

Show the children how to cut decorative edges and make fringes before they make a rakhi of their own. Encourage them to follow their designs by stapling a doily between two pieces of foil and decorating with shiny material or glitter.

Discussion
Explain that sisters tie rakhi around the wrists of their brothers. In return the brothers give them gifts such as a sari or money. It is a time when Hindu people think about caring for each other in a brotherly or sisterly way. Girls who don't have a brother might give a rakhi to a cousin or a close family friend. The word 'Raksha' means 'protection' and 'Bandhan' means 'to tie'. Discuss ways in which the group can be more friendly and caring.

The festival relates to a time when Krishna had a cut. His real sister took time to search for a bandage. In contrast, his adopted sister ripped her sari to form a makeshift bandage. He appreciated her kindness. Can the children think of ways in which they can be kind at home?

SPECIAL DAYS: DRAGON BOAT FESTIVAL
July/August Hindu festival, a time when people think about caring for each other in a brotherly/sisterly way. Gifts are exchanged and a sister will tie a rakhi around her brother's right wrist.

Follow-up activities
● Make a display consisting of the rakhi and children's suggestions for caring such as 'look after the animals' or 'help each other'.
● Look at other family celebrations such as baptisms and weddings. (Be sensitive to individual circumstances.)
● Tell the children the story of the Lord Vishnu giving Indra's wife a thread to tie around her husband's wrist. It protected him in his battle with the wicked King Bali.

Differentiation
Give younger children more direction and instruction. Encourage more experienced children to experiment with different materials.

ON THE CD-ROM
● Photograph of tying a rakhi
● Poem 'The Rakhi'

Autumn and winter

Find out about and celebrate a range of autumn and winter festivals, from the universally recognised festival of Harvest, to the winter celebrations of Eid, Divali, Hanukkah and Christmas.

World harvests

Food

themes for early years

STEPPING STONE
Gain an awareness of the cultures and beliefs of others.

EARLY LEARNING GOAL
Begin to know about their own cultures and beliefs and those of other people. (KUW)

ASSESSMENT
Observe the way in which children are able to contribute to discussions about different countries and beliefs.

What you need
Orange juice; chocolate; sugar; rice pudding; an orange; sugar cane; rice; map of the world; selection of books and pictures which show how foods grow.

What to do
Show the children the food items and ask them where they would expect to be able to buy the items. Trace the products back to their countries of origin. Use the books and pictures to find examples of growing rice, orange trees, sugar cane and cocoa beans. Find the countries of origin on the maps, for example: oranges – Spain, Israel; sugar – Jamaica; chocolate – Ghana, Brazil; rice – India, USA.

HARVEST
September/October
The date is determined by local conditions. A time of giving thanks for the harvest and one of the oldest of all festivals.

Ask the children which other countries they have experience of, either through visits they have made, relatives who live overseas or from watching television. Mark all of the countries mentioned on the map and indicate an import from that country if you know one.

Ask the children to have a look at home for foods that use ingredients originating in different countries. Mark these products and their countries of origin on the map too.

Discussion
Talk about harvest celebrations in different countries and religions such as the 'Crop Over' parties in sugar-growing areas of Jamaica, the Jewish Shavuot, and the yam harvest celebrated with music and food in West Africa. Traditionally in Japan the harvested rice was only eaten after the ceremonial processions and dances. In India the spring harvest is celebrated during the Holi (Hindu) and Baisakhi (Sikh) celebrations.

Follow-up activities
● Make a collection of food labels and highlight the countries of origin.
● Look at pictures of bread from around the world. Many countries have bread as the staple food but they are all different types.

ON THE CD-ROM
● Photograph of harvest display

Differentiation
Use more familiar foods with younger or less able children. Extend the range of foods used with more experienced children.

Art and craft

themes for early years

In the past

What you need
Internet access to find pictures of historic and current harvest scenes; large sheet of paper; wide variety of fabrics and papers; paints; scissors; adhesive; collage materials.

Preparation
Set out the materials for the children. Enlist their help in preparing the background to a collage on your display board (include a farmhouse, fields, both arable and pasture, narrow road, trees).

What to do
Look at the assortment of pictures you have gathered, paying particular attention to the features that are different when comparing the historical scenes to those of the present day. Directly compare the two sets of images and invite the children to tell you what they can see.

Show the children the prepared display background and explain that you are going to make a picture of harvesting in the past. Ask for suggestions on what add to it? Make a list of all their ideas, which might include: wagon and horses, haystack, pitch fork, scythe and sickle.

Work with the children to use the materials to make the ideas they have come up with. Assist them in getting the size in proportion but let them take the lead in deciding which materials to use. The emphasis is on encouraging all the children to take part rather than on producing a perfect picture. Keep the construction fairly simple, for example, paint a figure of a woman and add a fabric gathered skirt to give a 3D effect. Add sheep, cows and hens in the fields not being harvested and perhaps some birds and rabbits to complete the picture. Let the children make decisions about where features should be placed.

Discussion
Consider the pictures of harvest in the past. What do they notice? What would it feel like to be dressed like that? Can they see any evidence of electricity? What kinds of transport can they see? Can they imagine life without cars and televisions? Discuss the atmosphere at harvest time with all of the community being involved both in the work and in the Harvest celebrations afterwards. The last wagon would have been decorated and there would probably have been a large supper provided by the farmer's wife. The last piece of corn cut was traditionally made into a corn dolly.

Follow-up activities
- Visit a folk museum to look at old farming implements. Some museums have a loan service for educational use.
- Ask families and members of the community for any stories or photographs of harvest. Make simple corn dollies from straws.

Differentiation
Vary the techniques used according to the skills of the children.

STEPPING STONE
Begin to differentiate between past and present.

EARLY LEARNING GOAL
Find out about past and present events in their own lives, and in those of their families and other people they know. (KUW)

ASSESSMENT
Record the children's understanding of the past.

themes for early years

Harvest markets

What you need
On-screen harvest activity on the CD-ROM; samples of the fruit identified in the CD-ROM activity; card; a role-play market stall; fruit and vegetables for the stall (either real or imaginary); the rhyme 'The harvest' on page 84.

Preparation
Cut shapes from card for all of the fruit used in the on-screen activity. Prior to using the activity with the group demonstrate how to move each object to the appropriate place on the stall.

What to do
Share the rhyme 'The harvest' with the children and talk about the fruit and vegetables mentioned.

Show the samples of fruit and vegetables to the children and give them the opportunity to feel and smell each one. Are they always the same or does the size and shape vary? Ask each child to concentrate on one piece. Can they identify it when placed with the others? Can the children think of any other foods of similar appearance, for example, a banana and a plantain; a cucumber and a courgette. Let the children explore the fruit further with the role-play market stall.

Show the outlines of the fruit and vegetables on the on-screen activity to the group. Can they match the foods to the appropriate shape? Talk about the features as individual children attempt to match them. Involve the whole group by asking if they are correct and to name the food. Explain where each type of fruit is grown and how it is harvested (link this to 'World harvests' on page 35). Ask a small group of children in turn to complete the task on the CD-ROM.

Discussion
Discuss the way in which markets can be found in most parts of the world. Have the children been to any in a different area? Have they tried any foods that are new to them? Talk about the arrangement of foods on the stall with all of one variety being arranged together. Does size and shape matter in the arrangement?

Follow-up activities
- Take photographs of the selected fruit and use the pictures as a resource for games as well as to create a display.
- Visit a local market together.
- In discussion, relate the activity to people – we are all different in appearance but we are all humans.

Differentiation
Support children who are learning to click and drag on the computer. Ask confident children to extend their use of mathematical language by instructing other children.

STEPPING STONE
Show curiosity and observation by talking about shapes, how they are the same or why some are different.

EARLY LEARNING GOAL
Use language such as 'circle' or 'bigger' to describe the shape and size of solids and flat shapes. (MD)

ASSESSMENT
Observe the confidence and accuracy of children as they match the fruit to the shape. Note the language used and the computer skills displayed.

ON THE CD-ROM
- On-screen harvest activity
- Poem 'The harvest'

themes for early years

STEPPING STONE
Show curiosity, observe and manipulate objects.

EARLY LEARNING GOAL
Find out about, and identify, some features of living things, objects and events they observe. (KUW)

ASSESSMENT
Ask children to tell the story of the growth according to their sequences. Does it make sense?

How does produce grow?

What you need
The photocopiable sheet 'Harvest cards' on page 39; the song 'Ready for harvest' on page 80.

Preparation
Copy the photocopiable sheet onto card, colour in the pictures in appropriate colours and cut out the cards along the lines indicated. For more durability laminate the sheet before cutting it out.

What to do
Mix each of the four sets of cards (trees, lettuce, tomato plant and wheat). Select one set and show the children how to put them in order to depict the growth of an apple tree, a lettuce, some tomatoes or some wheat. Mix them up again and give one set to each child. Ask the children to rearrange the cards into the correct order of growth. Give each child the opportunity to try each set. Younger children may need to use fewer cards in their sequence to start with.

Sing the song 'Ready for harvest' together.

Discussion
Explain in a very simple manner that the sequences show the pattern of growth from a seed – plant – flower – fruit. Discuss the basic needs of light and water. How do other plants grow? For example, rice or pineapples? What about some of their favourite foods? Where and how do baked beans and chips 'grow'? What foods do we get from wheat? Does sugar really come from a plant? Explain that different foods are grown to suit the climate of different colours.

Follow-up activities
● Grow some mustard and cress and let all the children taste it.
● Grow the cress under different conditions (using varied light, water, and containers). Observe and discuss the differences.
● Grow plants from sprouting fruits and vegetables (try pineapple, potatoes, onions or carrots).
● Try growing plants from fruit pips and seeds such as avocado, apple, orange, date. These may require additional heat.
● Name the main parts of a plant: seed, stem, root, leaf and flower.

Differentiation
Extend the range of foods used as the children become more experienced.

ON THE CD-ROM
● Photocopiable sheet 'Harvest cards'
● Song 'Ready for harvest'

Harvest cards

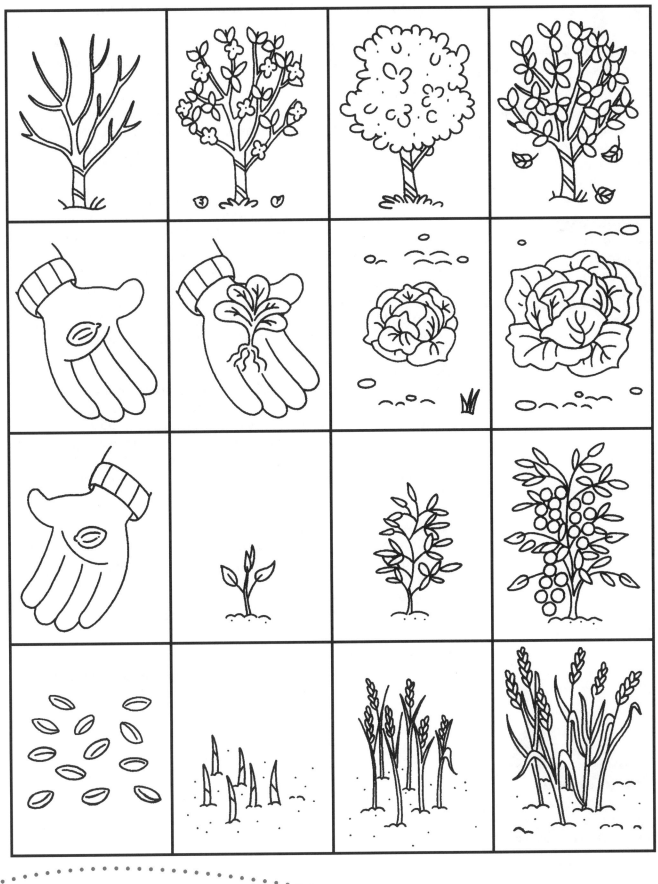

Construction and malleable materials

themes for early years

New moon

What you need
The photocopiable sheet 'The moon' on page 41; paper; scissors; glue; yellow crayons or felt-tipped pens; photographs of the moon in different phases.

Preparation
Copy the photocopiable page to provide one for each child. Enlarge one set to use as a demonstration.

What to do
Show the pictures of the moon to the children and see if they notice any differences between the images. Give a simple explanation of the moon going around the earth and explain that this is the reason for the changes in the shape of the moon. Talk about the order of the changes and use the enlarged photocopied pictures to illustrate this.

Demonstrate the way in which you would like the children to cut the shapes from their sheets, sequence them and then stick them onto background paper, colour and label the new moon. Ask the children to complete the same task and assist them with the ordering if necessary.

Discussion
Talk about the changes that children have observed or have noticed in the pictures. Why do they think that this happens? Encourage them to ask questions about the moon such as: *Why is it not visible on some occasions? Where does it go in the daytime? How long does it take to go from one phase to the next?* Explain that the festival of Eid starts with the sighting of the new moon. The festivities last for approximately three days.

Follow-up activities
● During the winter months encourage the children to have a look at the early evening sky and to describe the shape of the moon.
● Make a mobile to show the moon's phases and decorate the new moon with glitter.
● Read and discuss the rhyme 'Eid is coming' on page 86.

Differentiation
Give younger or less able children pre-cut shapes to sequence. Ask older or more able children to give an explanation for their ordering.

STEPPING STONE
Describe simple features of objects and events.

EARLY LEARNING GOAL
Find out about, and identify, some features of living things, objects and events they observe. (KUW)

ASSESSMENT
Record children's observations of the moon both during this activity and later.

EID-UL-FITR
Date is based on the lunar calendar and changes each year. Celebrated by Muslims at the end of Ramadan. Activities are also suitable for Eid-ul-Adha (at the end of Hajj – pilgrimage to Makkah).

ON THE CD-ROM
● Photocopiable sheet 'The moon'
● Poem 'Eid is coming'

The moon

● Cut out these phases of the moon and sequence them.

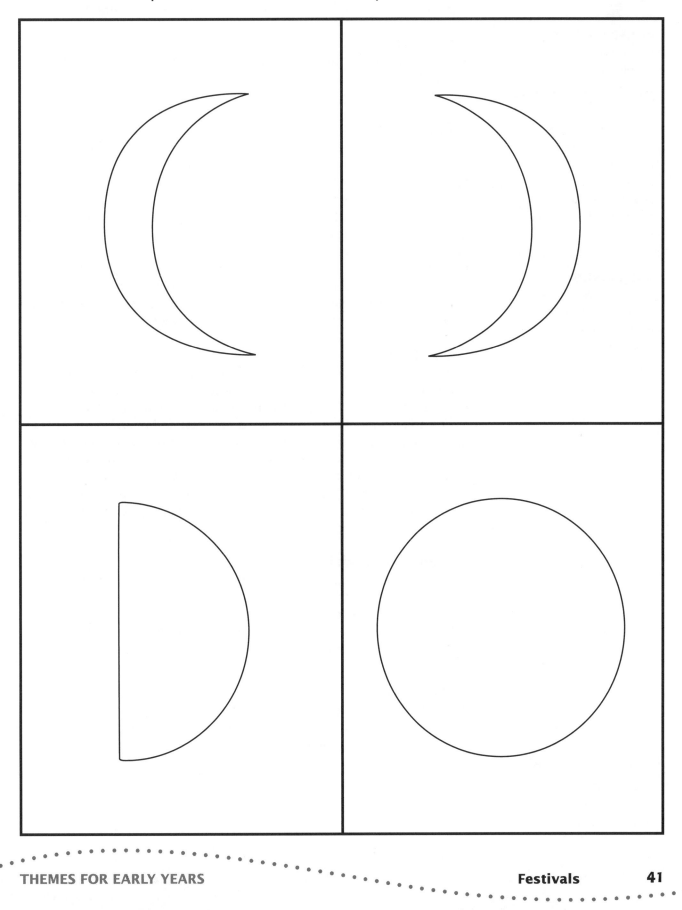

ICT

themes for early years

Make a poster

What you need
Access to a computer; on-screen Eid activity on CD-ROM; printing paper; crayons; copy of the words 'Eid Mubarak' in English and Arabic.

Preparation
Set up the computer ready for the children to use. Prepare an 'Eid Mubarak' poster of your own to show the group. Prepare copies of the Arabic writing if required.

What to do
Explain that the children are each going to make posters that say 'Happy Eid'. Show them the poster you have made and point out the completed patterned border.

Demonstrate how to use the on-screen activity on the CD-ROM to make a similar patterned border. Emphasise the way in which the pieces are placed symmetrically. Support children in using the CD-ROM to make their own patterns. While waiting for their turn invite the children to produce their own symmetrical patterns using crayons. Print the borders and write 'Eid Mubarak' (Happy Eid) or the Arabic version in the centre of each one. If printed in black and white ask the children to colour the shapes remembering to make a symmetrical pattern.

Discussion
Talk about the way you click and drag the shapes into place. Use the names of the shapes and include relevant vocabulary such as *same*, *opposite*, *next to* and *between*. Explain that the festival is a happy time after a solemn month when Muslim adults fast and pray. Eid-ul-Fitr is a great family celebration. The banner can be part of the decoration or it could be used to make a greeting card. Talk about occasions when the children enjoy celebrating with their families and friends. What kinds of decorations are used? Are any of them symmetrical? Explain that Arabic is used because it is the language of the Muslim Holy Book – the Qur'an. Show the children that it is written from right to left.

Follow-up activities
- Make other symmetrical patterns for cards, pictures of prayer mats or decorations.
- Look at and discuss other examples of symmetry.
- Provide other opportunities to use the click and drag technique.
- Use the border to decorate invitations to an Eid party.

Differentiation
Support younger or less able children by talking through the activity with them as they complete the programme. Show more confident children how to print their own work.

ON THE CD-ROM
- On-screen activity 'Eid Mubarak pattern'

Role-play

Anticipation

What you need
Space for the children to sit comfortably; paper; thick felt-tipped pens; adhesive or staples; pencils and crayons; the rhyme 'Eid is coming' on page 86; photograph of a mosque on the CD-ROM.

Preparation
Prepare an area to be used for a display, cut strips of paper to resemble banners (to hold the children's choice of descriptive words).

What to do
Sit the children around you and ask them about occasions when they have been waiting for something special, such as the night before a birthday or day out. Read and discuss the rhyme 'Eid is coming'. Ask individual children to tell you about their experiences and to describe their feelings and those of their family. Record the words they use such as 'excited', 'worried', 'can't sleep', on the paper strips in bold lettering. Some children might think of words later, these can still be shared with the group and added to the banners.

In small groups ask the children to act out their experiences before asking them to write and draw about their special occasion. These can then be grouped and recorded for the display such as 'Alex and Harprit wait for their birthdays', 'Jane and Ben wait to go on holiday'. When you prepare the display, arrange the banners so that they are distinctive and have a 3D effect.

Discussion
Talk about the different feelings that each family member might have for the same occasion. There might be concerns (about all the preparations; fear of flying) as well as the positive feelings of excitement. Extend the children's vocabulary and encourage them to be descriptive. Discuss the feelings of children waiting for Eid to commence: they have to wait for the new moon before celebrations can begin. Explain that the festival is celebrated with prayer, visiting the mosque (show and discuss the photograph), new clothes, cards, and visiting relatives.

Follow-up activities
- Use the display and encourage the children to use the words and phrases highlighted.
- Talk to a Muslim about the feelings associated with Eid and the other main festival of Eid–ul-Adha.
- Act the story of a family preparing for and celebrating Eid.

Differentiation
Prompt younger or less able children to remember and express their feelings. Encourage older or more able children to make their own written contributions to the display.

STEPPING STONE
Begin to use talk to pretend imaginary situations.

EARLY LEARNING GOAL
Use language to imagine and recreate roles and experiences. (CLL)

ASSESSMENT
Record the vocabulary used to show an understanding of anticipation.

ON THE CD-ROM
- Photograph of a mosque
- Poem 'Eid is coming'

themes for early years

STEPPING STONE
Initiate conversation, attend to and take account of what others say, and use talk to resolve disagreements.

EARLY LEARNING GOAL
Interact with others, negotiating plans and activities and taking turns in conversation. (CLL)

ASSESSMENT
Record the children's own version of the story.

Big book storytelling

What you need
Copy of 'The story of Divali' on page 94; pictures to illustrate the story (try schools' resource centre, a local library or the internet); access to a computer; paper; card; flame-coloured tissue and crêpe paper; paints and wool in any colours; thick felt-tipped pen.

Preparation
Use the paper and card to make a Big Book with a picture of a large diva on top.

What to do
Tell the story from the photocopiable sheet, using the pictures to illustrate it. When you have finished reading ask the children, as a group, to re-tell the story in their own words while an adult records their version. Ask an adult to type in the children's version of the story and to print it off in a large, clear font.

Help the children to decide which aspects of the story they will illustrate and let them make some large bold paintings. Stick these into the Big Book alongside the large print version of the children's text.

Show the children the photograph of the diva lamp and use this as a model to draw one on the cover of the book. To complete the book, add the title and decorate the cover by adding a tissue and crêpe paper flame to the diva.

Discussion
Talk together about welcoming people back who have been away for a long time. How would the children choose to be welcomed? Sikhs also celebrate Divali and visit the Gurdwara. Hindus like to visit the Mandir during the celebrations. Can the children think of any special occasions when they might visit a place of worship? What do they do there? (Remove shoes, sing, be a bridesmaid.) Talk about ways in which the festival is celebrated. People of both faiths visit relatives, decorate houses, exchange cards and gifts.

DIVALI
October/November
Hindus celebrate the triumph of good over evil, and Sikhs honour their sixth Guru, Hargobind. Homes and places of worship are decorated with diva lights.

Follow-up activities
● During the rescue of Sita, the monkeys built a bridge across to the island of Lanka. Try to design and make a long bridge using either reclaimed materials or construction sets.
● Act out the story as it is told.
● Tell the Sikh story relating to Divali.

Differentiation
Involve the younger or less able children in making the cover. Ask older or more able children to retell the story and include this in the book.

ON THE CD-ROM
● Photocopiable story 'The story of Divali'
● Photograph of a diva lamp

Construction and malleable materials

Making divas

What you need
Selection of egg cartons; Plasticine or play dough; yoghurt cartons; bases of plastic bottles; cardboard; coloured tissue paper; glitter; braid; sticky paper; glue; scissors; a decorated diva as a model or photograph of the diva on the CD-ROM; the rhyme 'Divali starts today' on page 87.

Preparation
Pre-cut flame shapes from cardboard and use this as a template to cut thin strips of tissue paper to make flames.

What to do
Look at the decorated diva or, if this is not available the photograph from the CD-ROM. Explain that the children are each going to make their own diva lamps and show them how to use the selection of craft materials to make a basic diva shape. Look together at the patterns on the example you have and use the decorative materials as imaginatively as possible to complete the divas.

Stick a small piece of Plasticine in each diva and make the flames by sticking tissue paper to both sides of the cardboard flame shapes (make sure they go vertically to resemble real flames).

Discussion
Talk about the importance of lights in this festival. The word Divali (also spelled Diwali or Deepavali) means 'a row or cluster of lights'. According to both the Hindu and Sikh stories, divas were used to welcome people. Traditionally, lamps are placed in windows and lit in the hope that Lakshmi, wife of Vishnu, will look in. She is thought to bring good luck – but only if the house is clean and tidy and all debts are paid. Read the rhyme 'Divali starts today' together to find out other ways in which Divali is celebrated.

Follow-up activities
● Decorate and light the diva lamps on the on-screen activity.
● Clean the role-play area and decorate it with the divas.
● Make some 2D pictures of divas. Display them effectively in silhouette against a tissue paper background and place them in a window.
● Look on the internet for pictures of the Golden Temple at Amritsar which looks particularly spectacular at Divali time.

Differentiation
Help younger or less able children to form the shape of the diva. Ask older or more able children to describe the patterns and textures created.

STEPPING STONE
Make three-dimensional structures.

EARLY LEARNING GOAL
Explore colour, texture, shape, form and space in two or three dimensions. (CD)

ASSESSMENT
Observe the way in which the children use colour, texture and shape.

ON THE CD-ROM
● On-screen activity 'Decorate the diva lamp'
● Photograph of a diva lamp
● Poem 'Divali starts today'

themes for early years

Rangoli patterns

What you need
Variety of coloured sticky-paper shapes; photocopiable page 47 'Pretty patterns', or other examples of rangoli patterns; scissors; glue; two pieces of contrasting paper approximately 20cm square per child.

Preparation
Fold one of the sheets into quarters, cut a curvy edge on the unfolded edge and open it out. Fold the contrasting sheet into quarters. Cut a design similar to one illustrated on the photocopiable sheet. Cut out the sticky-paper shapes. The amount of preparation required will depend on the cutting ability of the children, and many of the older children will be able to do some themselves. The variety of sizes, shapes and colours will depend on the age of the children.

What to do
Show the children examples of rangoli patterns – both commercially produced and handmade as well as those on the photocopiable. Explain that they are going to make their own smaller versions. Ask them to look closely at the patterns and see if they can identify the symmetry. Show them how to stick the patterned paper shapes on top of the square piece. Encourage them to decorate with sticky-paper shapes, trying to keep to a symmetrical pattern, either by colour or shape.

Discussion
Throughout the activity talk about placing one piece opposite another, aiming to have the same colour and shape. Explain that these patterns are made to decorate homes and Mandirs (Hindu places of worship) as a welcome for visitors during Divali. They can be made of chalk, sand, flour or rice, with freehand patterns usually being made by women. The designs might be geometric or based on flowers, fruit or trees. They can be rectangular, square or circular. When do the children decorate their homes? Do they ever have decorations outside their homes?

Follow-up activities
● Use the patterns to form a large wall display. The children can help to place them symmetrically.
● Make symmetrical patterns using alternative techniques such as paper folding and tearing, blot painting and tie-dye.
● Make a large group rangoli pattern using coloured chalk. Place it near the entrance to your room with a notice explaining that it is a welcome to visitors.
● Let the children colour the rangoli patterns on the photocopiable sheet and use these to create display borders or greetings cards.

Differentiation
Vary the amount of preparation according to the skills of the children. Encourage older children to make more complicated patterns.

Pretty patterns

● Colour in these Rangoli patterns.

themes for early years

Mango printing

What you need
Thick sponge; unbreakable containers for stamp pads; paints; mango; potato or other vegetable to print; wooden blocks; thick string; newspaper; printing paper; felt-tipped washable pens; aprons.

Preparation
Prepare the stamp pads by placing thick sponges in containers and soaking them in different coloured paints. Make the printing blocks in a mango shape. Use differing techniques: sponge cut to shape; vegetable cut to shape; thick string stuck to a wooden block; sponge shapes of different sizes stuck to a cardboard roll. Place the paper on a pad of newspaper to make a good printing surface.

What to do
Ask the children to wear protective clothing so that they can take part in this printing activity. Show them the mango and explain that many patterns in India are based on its shape as mango grows there. Demonstrate the techniques required to use all of the printing blocks. Give the children the opportunity to try each one with different colours. Emphasise the need to keep the colours separate.

When the children have experimented, give them the chance to have a new sheet to produce a final version. Allow the prints to dry, then ask the children to add more detailed patterns to the mango shape. If available, show them examples of mendhi patterns that are based on this shape.

Discussion
Explain that the shape is frequently used in patterns elsewhere, for example, the Paisley pattern in Scotland. Talk about the way that shapes are repeated in a pattern. Look at other examples of patterns and see if the children can identify the repeats. Each technique will produce a different outcome. Discuss the differences produced. Can the children suggest any changes that they could make?

Follow-up activities
- Use a print to make a greeting card for Divali.
- Make a border for a display or photograph frame.
- Print a design on fabric, which can then be used to make a doll's sari or skirt.
- Prepare a display using different patterns based on the mango shape.

Differentiation
Encourage the younger or less able children to experiment with printing and the use of colour. Ask older or more able children to discuss texture and pattern in greater detail.

STEPPING STONE
Work creatively on a large or small scale.

EARLY LEARNING GOAL
Explore colour, texture, shape, form and space in two or three dimensions. (CD)

ASSESSMENT
Observe the children's awareness of pattern, colour and texture.

Make a menorah

STEPPING STONE
Construct with a purpose in mind, using a variety of resources.

EARLY LEARNING GOAL
Build and construct with a wide range of objects, selecting appropriate resources, and adapting their work where necessary. (KUW)

ASSESSMENT
Observe the techniques and skills demonstrated in constructing the menorah.

What you need
Photograph of a hanukiah on the CD-ROM; examples or illustrations of other menorah; modelling materials; glue; scissors; box or wooden block; decorative materials; tissue paper; stiff card; modelling tools.

HANUKKAH
This eight-day Jewish festival of light commemorates the story of the Jews overcoming the Syrians and returning to their desecrated temple, it is a joyous family occasion.

Preparation
Collect examples of different menorah, cut two cardboard stars for each child, prepare the work area and the dough (or similar material).

What to do
Examine the different menorah especially the special one used for Hanukah (a hanukiah) which has a 'slave' candle and eight smaller ones. Explain that you would like the children to make one from card or dough. Ask them to look closely at the shape and decorations and consider how they can incorporate these ideas in their own work.

● Star of David: (see illustration)
   Carefully stick the two triangles together to form a star. Attach one point to a block to enable it to stand. Cut candles from card and attach these to the points. The 'slave' candle will be at the top. Use tissue paper to make the first flames. Others can be added on subsequent days.
   Decorate the menorah using a variety of materials and ideas.
● Modelling material:
   Allow the children to construct their own style.
Give them support to enable the structure to stand as necessary. Decorate the model in a variety of ways.
   Complete the session by sharing their experiences.

Discussion
Talk about the way in which the menorah is often placed on the windowsill with one candle being lit each night. It is a reminder of the time in Jewish history when the Temple had been destroyed. They sought to keep the eternal flame burning but there was very little oil. Miraculously it burned for eight days until help arrived.

Follow-up activities
● Make a display of 2D and 3D menorah designs.
● Find out about the story of Hanukkah and act it out as it is told.

Differentiation
All children can perform the same task but differentiate by the level of support given.

ON THE CD-ROM
● Film clip 'Lighting a hanukiah'
● Photograph of a hanukiah

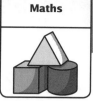
Maths

themes for early years

Dreidel game

What you need
Photocopiable sheet 'Dreidel board' on page 51; four counters of the same colour for each child; four base boards; stiff card; cocktail stick or pencil (to be used as a dreidel); example of a dreidel or an illustration of one.

Preparation
Use the photocopiable sheet to make the base board – complete each box on the sheet by adding a colour, shape or number, relevant to the group of children playing the game. Use stiff card to cut out a spinner, marked to correspond to the baseboard pictures.

What to do
Show the children the dreidel and explain that it is used by Jewish people when playing a game. Explain that they will be able to play it when they are older, but they are now going to learn a simpler version.

Explain the instructions for playing the game, pointing out that the emphasis is not on winning but playing together. To play the game each child places a counter on the start. They then take it in turns to spin the disc and place a counter on the matching shape. When a child has covered all four they move them to the menorah. The winner is the first child to reach the menorah having collected all the stages on the way.

Discussion
Talk about the dreidel game reminding Jewish people of something that happened a very long time ago when, although they were not allowed to read their Holy Writing, they could still play this game. Explain that the menorah is also very special and the eight candles are a reminder of the eight days it took to restore the Synagogue. Talk about taking turns and going first, second, third, fourth. Why do we take turns when playing games? Place the emphasis on playing together rather than on who wins or loses.

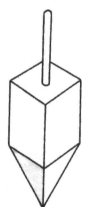

Follow-up activities
● Each child could make a game and take it home to play with their families and friends.
● Show the children a dreidel (or a picture of one) that would be used in Jewish homes. Older children can make one of their own.
● Make a collection of writing in different languages. Look, for example, on biscuit wrappings, electrical instructions or clothes' labels. Display and label them with the name of the language, and the name of the country/countries where it is spoken.

Differentiation
Mark the base board according to the mathematical needs of the children. For younger children, colour the lettering on the base board and the spinner to match.

Dreidel board

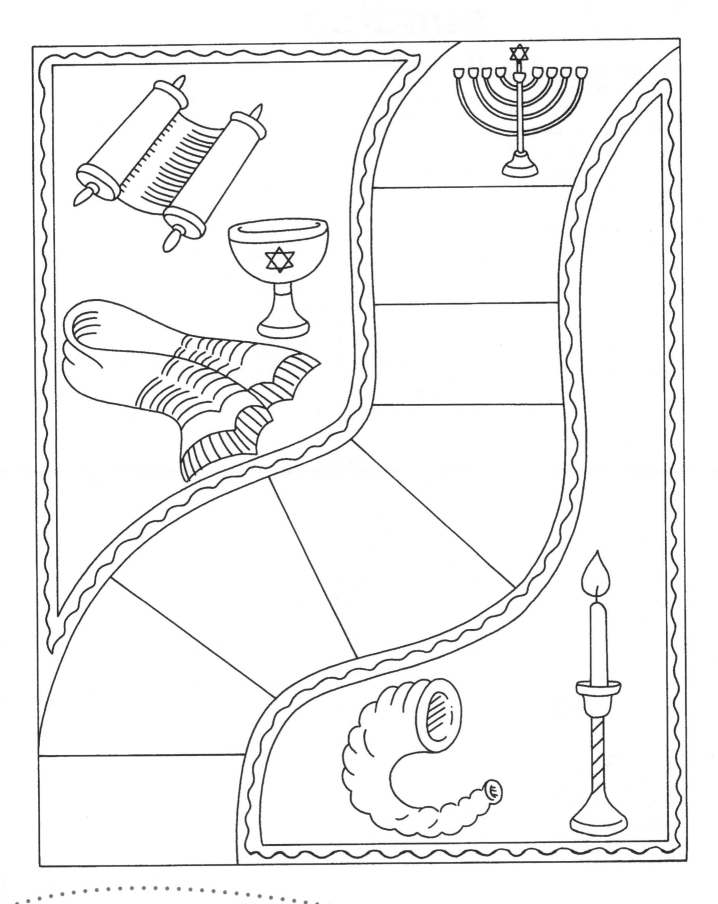

Maths

themes for early years

Light the candles

What you need
A hanukiah (the nine-branched candlestick, contact a local RE Resource Centre or synagogue); nine candles to fit the hanukiah; matches or a lighter (adult use only); photograph of a hanukiah on the CD-ROM; film clip 'Lighting a hanukiah' on the CD-ROM.

Preparation
Place the hanukiah in a place where it is safe but can be seen by all the children.

What to do
Watch the film clip together and explain that this activity of lighting the candles will take place eight times. If possible carry out this activity during the actual festival of Hanukkah. Within Jewish families it would take place before the evening meal, so perhaps before snack time, lunch or home time would be appropriate.

Ask the children to sit very quietly while an adult lights one candle. On the second day light two and so on. Use this as an opportunity to reinforce counting, add on one and so on. Divide the candles into two sets – those burning and those not. Will the sets be the same every day? Help the children to identify a pattern.

Discussion
Tell the children that it took eight days to restore the synagogue. Explain that in Jewish homes the candle would be alight for half an hour. Prayers would be said before lighting them. On each day children would receive a gift, usually money. It is a very special light that should not be 'used' in any way for work or reading. Discuss precautions that can be taken to ensure that candles are enjoyed safely.

Follow-up activities
- Make up a group prayer or rhyme of thanks. Talk about saying 'Thank you'. What would the children like to include? Share the 'Thank you' with the other members of the group.
- Make a matching card game. Give eight children three cards each (approximately 5cm × 8cm). Ask them to draw a child, a gift and a candle on three separate cards using bold colours. To play the game, place the cards face down on the table and let the children take turns to try to find a set of three cards.
- Using copies of the photocopiable sheet 'Add a flame' on page 53 invite the children to use collage materials to add a flame on each candle.

Differentiation
Concentrate on number names with the younger children. Ask older children to predict the following number.

Add a flame

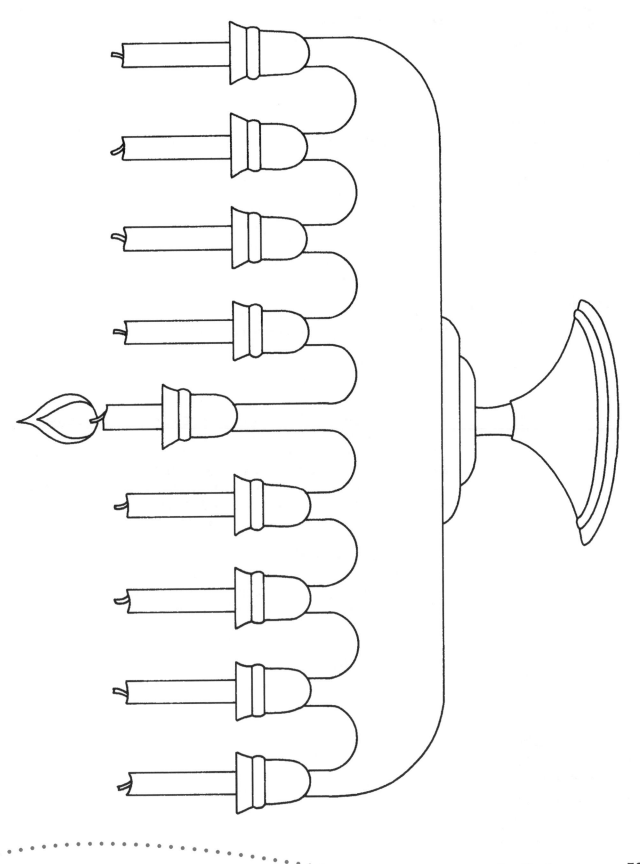

The Christmas story

themes for early years

STEPPING STONE
Express needs and feelings in appropriate ways.

EARLY LEARNING GOAL
Have a developing awareness of their own needs, views and feelings and be sensitive to the needs, views and feelings of others. (PSED)

ASSESSMENT
Observe the children's awareness of the feelings of others during the discussion.

What you need
Nativity set with models of a stable, manger, animals and characters in the story; a children's Bible (Luke 2); the photocopiable sheet 'Baby Jesus' on page 53.

CHRISTMAS
25 December Marks the birth of Jesus Christ, recognised by nativity plays, cribs and activities centred on the nativity story. Associated with gifts, lights, cards, food and Father Christmas.

What to do
Explain that you are going to tell the children a story that is special for Christians which comes from the Holy Bible. Show them the Bible and explain that it should be handled carefully.

Tell the children that you are going to tell them the story of the birth of a very special baby called Jesus. Tell the story of the Nativity using the stable, manger and characters at the appropriate times. Tell the children that it is because of Jesus' birth that we celebrate Christmas to remember his birthday. Sing a Christmas carol together such as 'Away in a manger'.

Use the photocopiable sheet 'Baby Jesus' on page 55 for the children to sequence the pictures and retell the Christmas story.

Discussion
Explain that 25 December is not the actual date of Jesus' birth as nobody is really sure when it was. In some countries Christmas is celebrated in January. How do the children celebrate their birthdays? Many Christians like to start the celebrations by going to church. Have any of the children been to church? Discuss their experiences. Think about people who find it difficult to celebrate Christmas such as old and lonely people, people who have to work or help others on that day. How can they celebrate? What can we do to let them know that they are remembered? Talk about the Wise Men taking gifts to Jesus.

Follow-up activities
- Learn other songs that tell the story of Christmas.
- Act out the story using simple props and costumes.
- Invite a representative of the local church to talk to the children about Christmas.

Differentiation
Reduce the number of pictures when sequencing the story with younger children. Ask older children to add captions to the pictures.

ON THE CD-ROM
- Photocopiable sheet 'Baby Jesus'

Baby Jesus

● Cut out the pictures and put them in the right order.

themes for early years

STEPPING STONE
Have a sense of self as a member of different communities.

EARLY LEARNING GOAL
Have a developing respect for their own cultures and beliefs and those of other people. (PSED)

ASSESSMENT
Observe the way in which children react to ideas and pictures that are new to them.

Artist's impression

What you need
Pictures of the Nativity; examples of art from different periods and cultures (look at Christmas cards and art books); books with Christmas stories from other countries; plastic bags or sheeting; crayons; paint brushes; different types of paper; felt-tipped pens.

Preparation
Plan possible questions to ask about the pictures. Cover pictures with plastic (opened-out bags or sheeting) fixed with sticky tape to protect them from art materials.

What to do
Show the children the pictures which you have gathered from a variety of sources, one at a time. Explain that, although the pictures are all different, they all depict the same story. Look first for the common features and characters. Who can they recognise in the pictures? Remind them of the Nativity story and see which pictures relate to different parts of it. Now see which parts they can identify as different? Encourage them to observe features such as the appearance of faces, types of clothes, halos, animals and stars.

Ask the children to each choose a picture, observe it, and then to produce their own version in a similar style. Show them the materials you have ready for use and encourage them to choose for themselves which they want to use. Emphasise the colours and characters rather than a 'perfect' reproduction. When they are complete, make a display of the children's work together with the original pictures.

Discussion
Compare the way people dressed in the pictures with present day clothes. Why do the children think that there are differences in the pictures if the story is the same? Is there a difference if the picture comes from a hot country? Do any of the pictures give any indication of how Christmas is celebrated in another country?

Follow-up activities
● Make a collection of old Christmas cards showing Christmas in the past. Either display them or make a group scrapbook. How do we know that they are in the past?
● Find out about Christmas in other countries. Many of the features on Christmas cards originated in different countries such as the poinsettia (Mexico and the Caribbean), the log (France), Santa Claus (USA), the decorated tree (Germany).

Differentiation
Differentiate by the selection of pictures used and the support given during discussion.

themes for early years

Family traditions

STEPPING STONE
Show interest in the lives of people familiar to them.

EARLY LEARNING GOAL
Find out about past and present events in their own lives, and in those of their families and other people they know. (KUW)

ASSESSMENT
Make a record of children's responses to past events. Do they understand the ideas of different places and different times?

What you need
Paper; art materials; scissors; sticky tape; writing materials; potatoes; paint; the rhyme 'This special day' on page 87; on-screen Chrismas activity on the CD-ROM.

Preparation
Demonstrate the on-screen Christmas jigsaw and talk about the family traditions depicted. Do they reflect the children's experiences? Write a letter to the children's families asking for any memories of how parents and grandparents celebrated Christmas in the past. Ask them to think about decorations, food, games, visitors and songs. Prepare a potato print to represent each category.

What to do
Share the replies that you receive with the whole group. Ask the children to record the responses in a variety of ways – copying writing, drawing, painting, reproducing decorations, cutting and sticking.

Cut out the responses and sort them into the separate categories such as 'decorations', 'food' and so on, and make them into separate books. To add interest, make each book in a relevant shape such as a tree or a present. Help the children to arrange their work in the books, and to use the potato prints to make decorative borders for their covers. Ensure that every child makes a contribution. Show the finished books to their families and thank them for their contributions.

Discussion
Talk about the replies you get and discuss how the customs are similar or different to present day celebrations? Were any of the memories from outside your area or from wartime? Talk about giving and receiving presents. Who would the children like to give a present to and what would it be? Discuss the friends and families who we visit during the celebrations. (Be sensitive to individual circumstances.) Say the poem 'This special day' together.

Follow-up activities
- Encourage the children to complete the jigsaw activity on the CD-ROM independently.
- Visit local shops to see their Christmas decorations.
- Find out about some of the stories attached to the pictures on Christmas cards such as the robin who fanned the flames to keep Baby Jesus warm and scorched his breast; the weeds that turned into poinsettias as the poor child gave her gift to the crib in Mexico.

ON THE CD-ROM
- On-screen activity 'Match the Christmas pictures'
- Poem 'This special day'

Differentiation
Limit the number of categories for younger children. Work with more mature children to find links and differences between responses.

Art and craft

themes for early years

Poinsettia Advent calendar

What you need

Poinsettia plant; old Christmas cards; backing paper in a colour to complement red and green; low level display board; photocopiable page 59 'Advent calendar'; scissors; adhesive materials; red, green and yellow paper and crayons; copy of the 'Advent calendar song' on page 79.

Preparation

Use the photocopiable sheet as a template to cut out 24 large and 24 small poinsettia shapes (either in red and green paper, or white paper for the children to colour using different shades and materials). Select appropriate cards to enable the children to cut out 24 scenes depicting different aspects of Christmas celebrations and the Christmas story. Cover the display board with backing paper.

What to do

Sing the 'Advent calendar song'. Talk to the children about the Advent calendar and decorations used at Christmas time.

Look at the poinsettia plant together and talk about the colours of the leaves. Ask the children to make up some poinsettia flowers for an Advent calendar by sticking a red flower shape on top of a green one. The centre can be made by colouring a circle or covering it with tiny tissue paper balls.

Ask the children to cut out the pictures on the Christmas cards very carefully. Stick these to the board either in a random way or so that the final display resembles a plant. Stick the poinsettias over the pictures using sticky tape or Blu-Tack. Number each one, with 24 being a picture of the scene in the stable if possible.

During Advent, remove one poinsettia each day to reveal the pictures. Place the removed flowers along the edge to form a border.

Discussion

Explain that the poinsettia is particularly associated with Christmas in the Caribbean area. Talk about there being different customs in different parts of the world. Discuss each picture as it is revealed. How is it associated with Christmas? Why is the stable scene number 24? Talk about the numbers involved. Which number will tomorrow be?

STEPPING STONE
Engage in activities requiring hand-eye coordination.

EARLY LEARNING GOAL
Handle tools, objects, construction and malleable materials safely and with increasing control. (PD)

ASSESSMENT
Observe the control shown by children as they cut the cards.

Follow-up activities
● Explain that 'Happy Christmas' can be written in different languages. Use some of these to decorate the board.
● Use the real poinsettia plant for the children to observe and make their own drawings.

Differentiation

Younger children may need to have lines drawn to direct their cutting. Ask older children to assist with the numbering. Encourage them to ask questions about the pictures as they are revealed

ON THE CD-ROM
● Photocopiable sheet 'Advent calendar'
● Song 'Advent calendar song'

Advent calendar

Maths

Who was first?

What you need
Copy of the 'Chinese New Year story' on page 95; the photocopiable sheet 'New Year race' on page 61; card; scissors.

Preparation
Copy the photocopiable sheet onto card and cut out the pictures to make cards; involve the children in this if they are able to help. Make enough copies for paired work.

What to do
Read the story of the Chinese New Year to the children. Remind them how the years were named according to the order the animals finished the race.

Show the cards to the children and discuss both the numerals and the animal names. Demonstrate the way they fit together in the correct order. Distribute a few cards to pairs of children and ask them to complete the sequence. Gradually increase the number of cards until they have a full set. The game can then be repeated with more cards and less support.

Discussion
Talk about the way that the argument was settled by using numbers that are always in the same order. It was a fair way to solve the problem. Discuss other examples where it helps us to know that numbers are in order, for example, on the telephone, on a list or the pages in a book. Use mathematical language as the game progresses, such as next, how many, first, second, and last.

Follow-up activities
- Place the first five cards in order. Remove one card and ask the children to name the missing numeral. Repeat the game with a different group of cards so that you do not always start with one.
- Use the cards as a number track to count forwards and backwards.
- Give cards to individual children and ask them to put themselves in the correct order. Vary the number of cards and start with different numerals.
- Ask the children to add a set of animal cards to the display on page 72.

Differentiation
Children requiring greater a challenge can develop their understanding of the language of ordinal numbers from first to twelfth or last. Those requiring additional support can be reminded of the story to complete the ordering and encouraged to both count and recognise numerals.

CHINESE NEW YEAR
January/February
Celebrated over 15 days, date determined by the new moon. Before the celebrations, homes are cleaned and decorated. Marked by street processions, fireworks and lion dancing.

STEPPING STONE
Begin to count beyond ten.

EARLY LEARNING GOAL
Say and use number names in order in familiar contexts. (MD)

ASSESSMENT
Observe the confidence displayed in finding the next numeral. Are the children using other clues too, for example, from the story? Note the mathematical language used by the children.

ON THE CD-ROM
- Photocopiable sheet 'New Year race'
- Photocopiable story 'The Chinese New Year story'

New Year race

1 Rat	2 Ox	3 Tiger
4 Rabbit	5 Dragon	6 Snake
7 Horse	8 Ram	9 Monkey
10 Cockerel	11 Dog	12 Pig

Art and craft

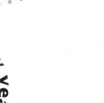

themes for early years

Good luck!

What you need
Glue; scissors; sticky tape; twigs; yoghurt pots; Plasticine; stiff paper; contrasting fabric; pre-cut frames; pink tissue paper; paper; paint, decorative papers and fabrics, sequins, glitter and gift wrap all in red, gold and yellow; gold braid.

Preparation
Prepare greeting card frames and prepare sheets for Lucky Bags. Follow the instructions below to make an example of each of the four items. Show these to the children and explain that, in four groups, they are going to make their own decorations using these basic designs, but decorating them as they like.

What to do
● **Lucky bags** – cut out a lucky bag outline. Show the children how to fold it, slowly and carefully. Glue the edges and stick down to form a lucky bag. Invite them to make a decoration, such as blossom, cut paper design, gold pattern, or the animal for the year, and to stick this to the centre of the bag.
● **Blossom trees** – decorate the yoghurt pots. Push a piece of Plasticine into the base of each pot, large enough to support some twigs. Tear pink tissue paper into pieces approximately 6cm square and crumple the centre of the paper to form flower shapes. Stick the blossom to the twigs and stand the 'blossom trees' in the decorated pots.
● **Greeting cards** – fold the card in half. Paint stems and pink blossom on the contrasting fabric. When dry, stick the painting to the outside of the card. Cover with the pre-cut frame and stick in place. On the inside, write 'Happy New Year' or 'Kung hey fat choy'.
● **Banner** – copy the Chinese greeting (above) onto yellow paper and cut out. Stick it on to the centre of a red piece of paper. Decorate the border in a variety of ways, such as with gold braid, small flowers cut from gift wrap, small pink blossom, or glitter.

Discussion
Discuss the way in which homes are thoroughly cleaned before being decorated with symbols of good luck such as banners, peach blossom, lions and dragons. People exchange cards and give children 'lucky money' from both lucky bags and branches hung with money. Do the preparations remind the children of any other festival preparations?

Follow-up activities
● Make lanterns from red and gold gift wrap around a cardboard tube covered with yellow paper.
● Make a Chinese New Year display, see page 72.
● Sing the song 'Chinese New Year' on page 75.

Differentiation
Differentiate by the level of adult support given. Discuss using 3D effects with the older children.

themes for early years

Sound

Lion dance

What you need
Large space; one hoop for each pair of children; tambourine (optional); CD player and suitable music; the 'Chinese New Year story' on page 95; the rhyme 'Chinese lion dance' on page 88; Chinese lion dance film clip on the CD-ROM.

Preparation
Tell the story of the animals' race across the river from the 'Chinese New Year story'. Watch the film clip of lion dancing together, and point out to the children how the head is held. Place the hoops in strategic places around the room so that the children can obtain them quickly and easily.

What to do
Start with a warm-up including activities in which the children must obey commands such as stop, go, change direction, and make movements that are high/low, fast/slow, and large/small. Use the tambourine to indicate a change or instruction.

Remind the children of the story and ask them to think how each animal would move. Experiment with different movements for the rat, ox, rabbit, snake, monkey, cockerel and dragons. Ask them to each choose one animal and to concentrate on the actions for that animal.

Ask the children to recall the video of lion dancing, and to try to reproduce the movements while you play some appropriate music. Tell them to share a hoop with a partner and to experiment with lion dancing using the hoop as the lion's head. Let half the group watch the others perform their dance, and then repeat with the other group.

Discussion
Explain that lion dancing is just one of the ways that the Chinese New Year is celebrated with processions where the dancing is accompanied by drums, gongs and symbols. Traditionally, the lions accompany a huge dragon as it dances along the road. Some shops and houses hang money (wrapped in red) from upstairs windows. The dancers then 'climb' up to collect it. It is hoped that the music will chase away evil spirits and that the dancing will encourage good luck during the following year. Talk about working together and taking turns.

Follow-up activities
● Encourage the children to accompany their movements with musical instruments.
● Decorate the hoop to resemble the head and use a decorated hoop for the body.
● Encourage the children to complete the on-screen activity 'Make a Chinese dragon'.

Differentiation
Work in smaller groups with younger children and give them additional encouragement to take part. Ask older children to 'perform' in front of an audience.

STEPPING STONE
Move in a range of ways, such as slithering, shuffling, rolling, crawling, walking, running, jumping, skipping, sliding and hopping.

EARLY LEARNING GOAL
Move with confidence, imagination and in safety. (PD)

ASSESSMENT
Observe the children as they move around the room. Are they aware of others? Do they use their imaginations?

ON THE CD-ROM
● Film clip 'Chinese lion dance'
● On-screen activity 'Make a Chinese dragon'
● Photocopiable story 'The Chinese New Year story'
● Poem 'Chinese lion dance'

Patron saints

What you need:

Flags: fabric, canes, ribbon, glue, felt-tipped pens; photocopiable page 65 'Saints' days'; poem 'Let's celebrate' on page 90. St David: paper, brushes, yellow and green paint, daffodils. St Patrick: large potatoes, thick green paint, paper or fabric. St George: waste materials, red paint, masking tape, red paper or fabric. St Andrew: badge backing, small pieces of heather, scissors, clear sticky-backed plastic.

> **SPECIAL DAYS: PATRON SAINTS**
> Each country of the UK has its own saint; each has a story, a flag and its own individual way of celebrating.

Preparation

For the flags, cut canes and fabric to size. Prepare copies of the photocopiable sheet for the children to copy, colouring in the four flags as a reference. St Patrick: cut shamrock shapes in the potatoes. St Andrew: make badge backs with card and safety pins.

What to do

Explain that each country has a specific saint associated with it. These were all real people who spread the Christian message many years ago. Each saint has their own special day.

Make a flag to celebrate the saints' days by fixing fabric to a garden cane, using the photocopiable page as a reference. Make the crosses with ribbon. Children can draw their own Welsh dragon with red felt-tipped pen. Decorate your room with the flags.

For each saints' day arrange a different activity:
- St David (1 March) : make observational paintings of daffodils, talk about the shape and colour as the children paint.
- St Patrick (17 March): make green potato prints based on a shamrock design. Use these to make a wall decoration or place mat.
- St George (23 April): use the recycled materials to make one large dragons. Talk about which materials and textures are appropriate for different parts. Involve all the children in painting it red.
- St Andrew (30 November): use a little glue to stick the heather to the badge. Cover with clear sticky-backed plastic.

Gather the children together to share the rhyme 'Let's celebrate'.

Discussion

Who are the modern saints? Who are our role models? Talk about people who are good to us and help us. Encourage children to ask questions about the stories and celebrations.

> **Follow-up activities**
> - Act out the relevant story to an invited audience. Decorate the invitations and the room according to the saint.
> - Make cards for family and friends who celebrate the saints day.

Differentiation

Vary the amount of preparation and support given according to the skills of the children

Saints' days

Flag of St David

Flag of St Patrick

Flag of St Andrew

Flag of St George

Construction and malleable materials

themes for early years

Janmashtami

What you need

Boxes; fabric; tissue paper; cover for the completed cradle; string; scissors; sticky tape; decorative materials; blue modelling clay; copy of the song 'Janmashtami' on page 81.

SPECIAL DAYS: JANMASHTAMI August/September Date varies. Celebration of Lord Krishna's birthday.

Preparation

Make the structure for the cradle from materials available in the setting, such as construction toys. Alternatively, arrange for them to be hung from the ceiling or on a string across the room. Cut circles from tissue paper.

What to do

Explain that you are going to prepare for a celebration that is very important to Hindus – Lord Krishna's birthday or Janmashtami. Use the fabric pieces to loosely line the inside of the box. Make the flowers by squeezing the centre of tissue paper circles, using two together or fringing the edge to vary the flowers. Attach the flowers to the outside of the basket with sticky tape. Additional decorations can be added such as glitter, sequins or pieces of tinsel.

Make four holes in the box, thread the string through them, and tie the strings to the pole. Make a small doll from blue modelling material to fit the cradle. Lord Krishna is usually illustrated with blue skin so this would be appropriate. Place the doll in the cradle and cover it with a cloth. Uncover it on the day of the festival. Gather around the cradle and sing the song 'Janmashtami' together.

Discussion

Explain that this is a very happy festival. Devout Hindus will often fast for 24 hours prior to the occasion and read from the Scriptures. Temples, and sometimes homes, will be decorated with tinsel, lights and glitter. The focal point will be the covered cradle. There is a great feeling of anticipation as families wait to uncover the cradle at midnight and see the baby. The celebrations then begin. Flowers and sweets are placed around the rocking cradle.

Follow-up activities
● Discuss how the children feel when waiting for a special time (see the activity 'Leaving home' on page 28).
● Find out if any of the children's families are Hindus. If so, ask them to discuss their memories of the festival and the importance of Lord Krishna.

Differentiation

Ask older children to discuss improvements that could be made to the structure. Work closely with younger children as they decorate their boxes.

STEPPING STONE
Construct with a purpose in mind, using a variety of resources.

EARLY LEARNING GOAL
Build and construct with a wide range of objects, selecting appropriate resources, and adapting their work where necessary. (KUW)

ASSESSMENT
Observe the children's skills and note their suggestions for improvement.

ON THE CD-ROM
● Song 'Janmashtami'

Ethiopian New Year

STEPPING STONE
Join construction pieces together to build and balance.

EARLY LEARNING GOAL
Select the tools and techniques they need to shape, assemble and join materials they are using. (KUW)

ASSESSMENT
Observe the skills used by children as they construct the star.

What you need
Black backing paper; glue; red, green and gold glitter; for each star: six split pins and two strips of red, green and gold card approximately 10cm by 1.5cm; photograph of Ethiopian New Year on the CD-ROM; song 'Ethiopian New Year' on page 82.

Preparation
Cut the strips and round the ends.

What to do
Consider ways to construct the star. Take three strips, one in each of the three colours. Fix them together with split pins, or similar, to form a triangle. To make the second triangle join two different colours together and weave these through the first triangle so that they only cross different colours. Weave the third piece through and join with split pins. Position the triangles to form a Star of David and stick in position.

Dot with glue and sprinkle with glitter. Make a border around the display paper by sprinkling red, green and gold glitter around the edge. Display the completed stars on the black background.

Gather together to sing the song 'Ethiopian New Year'.

Discussion
Explain that many of the Rastafarian traditions are associated with Ethiopia and Jamaica. The colours in the star are all in the Ethiopian flag and symbolise blood (struggle), the sun and the earth. The other symbol of Rastafarianism is the Lion of Judah. Show the photograph on the CD-ROM to the children and discuss. Festivals are generally celebrated by friends and families gathering together for exhibitions, drumming, dancing and food. Talk about the music that might be played during the festival. The music of Bob Marley and reggae grew out of the tradition of Rastafarian drumming and chanting. Discuss the food that might be eaten: strict Rastafarians only eat natural and organic food – often vegetarian and definitely not pork.

SPECIAL DAYS: ETHIOPIAN NEW YEAR
11 September Rastafarian New Year. Celebrated in family and community groups by eating, drumming and dancing, as well as talks and films about their faith.

Follow-up activities
- Make some food that is suitable for Rastafarians to eat such as banana bread, fruit punch, yam, plantain or cho-cho.
- Make home-made drums and decorate them with black, red, gold and green.
- The festival takes place very near the new school year; discuss ways to mark a new year and a new start.

Differentiation
Vary the amount of adult support given. Encourage more confident children to choose their own materials and equipment.

ON THE CD-ROM
- Photograph showing Ethiopian New Year
- Song 'Ethiopian New Year'

themes for early years

STEPPING STONE
Negotiate space successfully when playing racing and chasing games with other children.

EARLY LEARNING GOAL
Move with confidence, imagination and in safety. (PD)

ASSESSMENT
Observe the control and coordination shown by children. Make particular note of areas of development.

Role play

Sukkot

What you need
Large sheet of plain paper; Blu-Tack; photograph of a family in a sukkot on the CD-ROM; copy of the rhyme 'Palm, myrtle and willow' on page 83.

Preparation
Prepare a pencil sketch showing the main features of your room including the window, door, tables, role-play area, book area and sand tray. Make copies for the children to use. Divide the children into groups of six.

What to do
Tell the children that you are going to take a walk around the room and that you would like them to follow you in a procession.

The route could be something like: around the sand tray, between the window and the table, through the role-play hospital, in front of the bookshelf and past the door.

Now ask them to think of another route that they could take. Let them use the sketch to help describe their route. When they have made a final decision, let them record it on their copy of the sketch.

Repeat the activity with other groups of children and compare ideas. Children can follow the routes planned by another group. Encourage them to move carefully around the room avoiding furniture and people.

SPECIAL DAYS: SUKKOT
September/October
Jewish festival celebrating the harvest, and commemorating the time when Jewish people were protected in the wilderness by making temporary shelters to have their meals and rest.

Discussion
Explain that at the end of the festival the Torah is carried in procession around the synagogue. The festival itself, which takes place in late September, early October, is a reminder of the 40 years in which the Jewish people travelled in the wilderness and lived in temporary shelters. To remember this time, Jewish people build temporary shelters either at home or at the synagogue. Show the children the photograph of a family inside the shelter. Discuss the decoration. Share the rhyme, 'Palm, myrtle and willow'. Talk about the importance of having a route or plan. Have any of the children seen adults using a plan or a map? Talk about the use of the terms such as 'between', 'behind' and so on.

Follow-up activities
● Make a temporary shelter from a strong cardboard box. Make the roof from branches and leaves. Decorate it with pictures of fruit and add dolls' house furniture.
● Make a temporary shelter in the home corner.
● Tell stories that involve a route such as *Rosie's Walk*, Pat Hutchins (Picture Puffin).

ON THE CD-ROM
● Photograph of a family in a sukkot
● Poem 'Palm, myrtle and willow'

Differentiation
Encourage more confident children to take the lead and plan their own route. Encourage younger children to follow instructions carefully and avoid touching anything.

Sound

themes for early years

Guru Nanak's birthday

SPECIAL DAYS: GURU NANAK'S BIRTHDAY
November (although he was born in April). Guru Nanak started the Sikh religion and this is one of the most important days in the Sikh year.

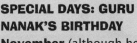

STEPPING STONE
Relate and make attachments to members of their group.

EARLY LEARNING GOAL
Form good relationships with adults and peers. (PSED)

ASSESSMENT
Observe children in their relationships with each other.

What you need
Space to sit in a circle.

What to do
Join the children to sit together in a circle and explain that you would like them to talk to the person next to them about someone who has been kind to them. They need to listen carefully to each other because they are then going to be asked to share what they have heard with the rest of the group.

Think together about ways that we can all be kind to each other. Ask each child to think of something that they can do to be helpful either at home or in the group.

Start with the child next to you, ask them to say what he or she can do. The next child repeats this and adds what he or she can do. Continue around the circle until it comes back to you and you have to repeat what each child can do.

Discussion
Explain that Guru Nanak believed that everyone is equally important. It doesn't make any difference how rich you are – you should still be kind and thoughtful. The free kitchens in Sikh Gurdwaras are based on his teaching: everyone helps and everyone shares. He was a very kind man who is reputed to always have had time to listen. He lived at a time when there was considerable conflict in India and it was his greatest wish to have peace. Guru Nanak is very special to Sikh people and you will often find pictures of him in their homes and Gurdwaras. Who is special to the children? Do they have photographs of special people? During the celebrations, the Holy Book (the Guru Granth Sahib) is read continuously from start to finish and the Golden Temple at Amritsar is illuminated. The celebrations take place in November. Talk about the way that families might celebrate and read the rhyme 'Guru Nanak's birthday' on page 88 together.

Follow-up activities
● Tell stories of people who have been kind and helpful such as Florence Nightingale, Mary Seacole and Mother Teresa.
● Make a wish for someone.
● Think of ways to make new children feel welcome in your group.
● Play cooperative games.

Differentiation
Give younger children suggestions and prompts. Work with older children to produce a list of ways to help each other.

ON THE CD-ROM
● Poem 'Guru Nanak's birthday'

Sound

themes for early years

Pancake Day

What you need
Selection of decorative and craft materials; thread; metal bottle tops; large tin; dried peas or rice; tins with lids; lengths of dowel; metal spoons; cooling rack; cardboard tubes; bells; string; paper plates; open boxes; elastic bands; yoghurt pots or paper cups; copy of the rhyme 'Carnival for Mardi Gras' on page 85.

SPECIAL DAYS:
PANCAKE DAY
Day before Ash Wednesday, beginning of Lent. Shrove or Fat Tuesday ('Mardi Gras') is an opportunity to eat up foods high in fat before Lent. Celebrated in many communities with carnivals.

Preparation
Make holes in the metal tops, lids and cardboard rolls. Watch the film of the carnival parade and explain that you would like the children to make their own instruments.

What to do
Let the children choose what instruments they want to make. Assist them in making the basic instrument but give them the opportunity to individualise their instruments by making simple adjustments and varying the decorations. Choose from these:
- **Shakers and rattles** – make from metal bottle tops, tins, yoghurt pots, paper plates and dried peas or rice.
- **Scrapers** – rub a spoon across a cooling rack or similar bumpy surface.
- **Cardboard shaker** – tie bottle tops or bells to the top of a tube.
- **Tambourine** – make holes around a paper plate. Tie bottle tops or bells around the plate.
- **Stringed instruments** – place several elastic bands around open boxes, vary the tension to give different sounds.

When all of the instruments are completed, choose a happy song that is familiar to all of the children and sing it with an instrumental accompaniment. Read the rhyme 'Carnival for Mardi Gras' and encourage the children to join in the chorus.

Discussion
Talk about the connections between carnivals and Pancake Day. Explain that they are both associated with enjoying yourself before the fasting period of Lent. Local customs developed across Europe such as pancake races in Olney (Buckinghamshire) and eating pretzels in parts of Germany. One of the most famous celebrations was the Carnival. The tradition was taken to part of the Caribbean and southern USA. This eventually led to steel band music and the present day carnivals.

Follow-up activities
- Make and eat pancakes. Try different fillings.
- Listen to the music of a steel band.

Differentiation
Vary the amount of support given as the chilren make their instruments. Encourage more confident children to choose their own materials.

STEPPING STONE
Try to capture experiences and responses with music, dance, paint and other materials or words.

EARLY LEARNING GOAL
Express and communicate their ideas, thoughts and feelings by using a widening range of materials, suitable tools, imagination and role play, movement, designing and making, and a variety of songs and musical instruments. (CD)

ASSESSMENT
Record the children's reactions to the instruments and their discussion comments.

ON THE CD-ROM
- Film clip of a carnival.
- Poem 'Carnival for Mardi Gras'

Displays

Creating colourful, purposeful displays helps to promote an interesting and exciting atmosphere that can play a valuable role in improving the children's learning environment and in promoting enthusiasm for a theme or topic. Displays not only reassure children how much we value their work but also demonstrate skills to parents, carers and visitors.

Divali

DISCUSSION
Talk about the way in which rangoli patterns are used as a welcome in doorways during the Divali festival. Discuss alternative ways to make them using chalk, powder or rice. Discuss symmetry at home or in the street. Experiment with a mirror by drawing simple shapes and examining the reflection in the mirror.

What you need
Board covered with a dark background; large sheet of paper; coloured chalks; small pieces of paper in different shapes and colours; glue; children's patterns; small unbreakable mirrors; fabric table-covering such as a sari.

Preparation
Fold the large sheet of paper into quarters. Fold along the diagonal to form eight sections. Cover the table with fabric.

What to do
Colour each section using the coloured chalks so that opposite sections are the same colour. Position the small pieces of coloured paper so that they form a symmetrical pattern. Take care to match shape, colour and size. When complete, fold the sheet of paper along the axis, and cut it to form an interested shape around the children's patterns. Mount the picture on the backing sheet.

Write the heading in large lettering and decorate with chalk. Place this in a prominent position. On a second sheet record the children's descriptions of how they were made. Display the children's own patterns on a table and place the mirrors along the axis.

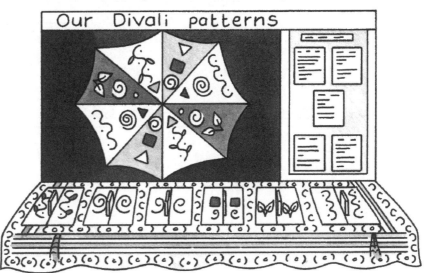

Chinese New Year

What you need

Display board covered with gold or yellow backing paper; red border; table draped with red, yellow or gold fabric or paper; items made by the children and contributed by families; labels and marker pens; glue; letter to families; mounting paper.

Preparation

Cover the table and board. Write to families to inform them of the display and invite them to contribute.

What to do

Talk about the composition of the display with the children. Explain that their hand-made items will be displayed alongside those lent by families. Demonstrate that, with limited space, only a few of their pieces can be displayed. Involve some of the children in making choices but explain that all of their work is valued. Make clear labels and a heading. Read these with the children. Involve children in mounting, arranging and labelling materials – including those on short-term loan.

DISCUSSION

Explain that red and gold are colours traditionally associated with the festival. Streets, shops and homes would be decorated with good luck symbols. Discuss ways in which families decorate homes for special occasions.

May Day

What you need
Two tables of different heights; luxurious-looking fabric or paper; large number of white or pastel-coloured paper flowers made from tissue paper; real flowers in two small unbreakable vases; memorabilia of past May Days; books about May Day; dolls to dress as the May Queen and May King (the king is optional); one or two small chairs, fabric to drape over the chairs, a copy of the rhyme 'The Maypole rhyme' on page 84.

Preparation
Cover the background and tables with the fabric or paper.

What to do
Shape the background into a semi-circle and edge it with paper flowers. Cover the chairs with the fabric and decorate with flowers to make a throne. Dress the dolls in their 'best' clothes and add flowers in their hair. Place the thrones towards the back of the higher table. Position the vases of real flowers on either side in a safe position.

Stand the books and memorabilia on the bottom table as the children bring them in. Add a copy of the rhyme 'The Maypole rhyme' on page 84. Involve the children in making labels to explain the source of each item.

DISCUSSION

Talk about how and why May Day is celebrated. Discuss the items and share memories of May Day in the past. Talk about the photographs. What are the clothes and cars like? How are the people celebrating? Was anyone wearing special clothes? Are the hairstyles any different from now? What artefacts would the children like to keep to remind them of special days?

Children's Day

What you need

Backing paper for the children's iris paintings; paper or fabric for the table; print of the Van Gogh painting *Irises* (optional); vase of irises; paper; bowls or plates with examples of healthy food or pictures of healthy food; canes; paper plates; paper cut into fish shapes (large enough for the fishes' mouths to fit around half of the plate); pieces of tissue paper; glue; sticky tape; scissors; Plasticine (optional).

Preparation

Cover the board and table with paper or fabric. Select children's paintings and mount or double-mount them. Make any paintings that will not be included in this display into a book, or add them to other work on the theme of Children's Day.

What to do

Arrange the paintings on the wall together with the Van Gogh print. Place the food on the table (or pictures of healthy food if actual food is not available or practical). Involve the children in making labels for the food to include a brief explanation of why that food is good to eat. Place the vase of irises in a safe position. Make the replicas of carp kites by cutting the centre from paper plates to leave a circular rim. Decorate two fish-shaped pieces with scraps of tissue paper, and stick the two pieces together by overlapping the sides and forming a circular mouth.

Attach the mouth to the plate rim with the sticky tape. Add the stick and fix to the table. (It might be helpful to stand the cane in a small piece of Plasticine). Write a short explanation of the reasons why irises and carp are associated with the festival and add these to your display.

DISCUSSION

Explain that at this time gardens are traditionally decorated with carp kites. The carp is chosen as it is thought to have the qualities of strength and determination, and is full of power and energy. The leaves of the iris are a reminder of the sword of the samurai warrior. The emphasis on eating food also fits with the theme of being strong in mind and body. How do the children try to keep their bodies fit and healthy? What can they do to keep healthy? Talk about healthy eating and foods that should only be eaten in small quantities, such as chocolates and cakes.

Chinese New Year

D

This is Chin-ese New Year, time to cel-e-brate.

A **D**

Clean the house and buy some flowers to de-cor-ate.

Write some New Year greet-ings, cook a spe-cial meal.

A **D**

Then at night the fire-works fizz and bang and squeal.

2. Underneath my pillow
Sweets in bag of red
Given by my parents
While I slept in bed.
I'll put on my new clothes
This day I'll enjoy
Greet my friends and family
Say 'Kung hey fat choy!'

Hazel Hobbs

Passover

Fm **A♭** **C** **Fm**

We ce-le-brate the Pass-o-ver with Se-der, prayers and sing-ing. While

E♭ **A♭** **E♭** **A♭**

food we are shar-ing, give thanks for God's car-ing. Re-

Fm **A♭** **C** **Fm**

mem-ber how he saved our peo-ple all those years a-go.

Hazel Hobbs

Dragon boat race

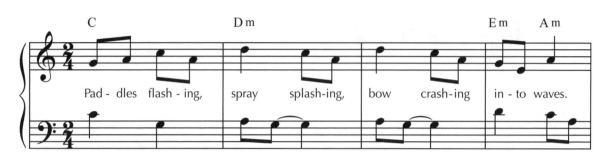

Paddles flash-ing, spray splash-ing, bow crash-ing in-to waves.

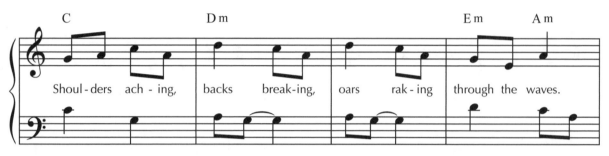

Shoul-ders ach-ing, backs break-ing, oars rak-ing through the waves.

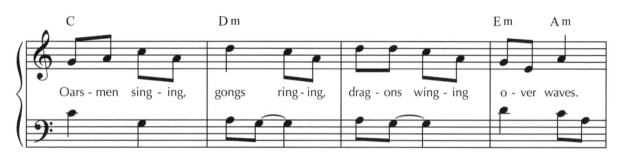

Oars-men sing-ing, gongs ring-ing, drag-ons wing-ing o-ver waves.

Gentle, flowing

Wat-er rip-ple, fish nib-ble, Ch'u Yuan rest be - neath the waves.

David Moses

Holi time

It's HO- LI eve, time to light the fires, then the fes - ti - val can be - gin ____ . We

give our thanks for the har - vest time and the food we've gath - ered in ____ . Let's

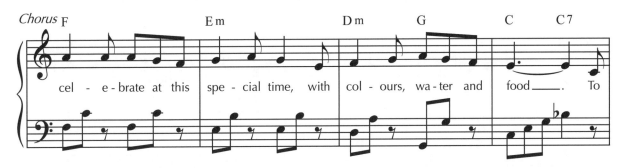

Chorus cel - e - brate at this spe - cial time, with col - ours, wa - ter and food ____ . To

show us all of a long time a - go, when e - vil was con - quered by good ____ .

2. It's HOLI day
Time to have some fun
With our neighbours, family and friends.
We'll play some tricks
And we'll all get wet!
And we hope it will not end.

Chorus

Peter Morrell

Five brave men

Spoken:
Many years ago, in the town of Anandpur, Guru Gobind Singh told the people to prepare. So they stood outside his tent and they listened to his words, when he asked them if they would die for him they wished they hadn't heard. THEN...

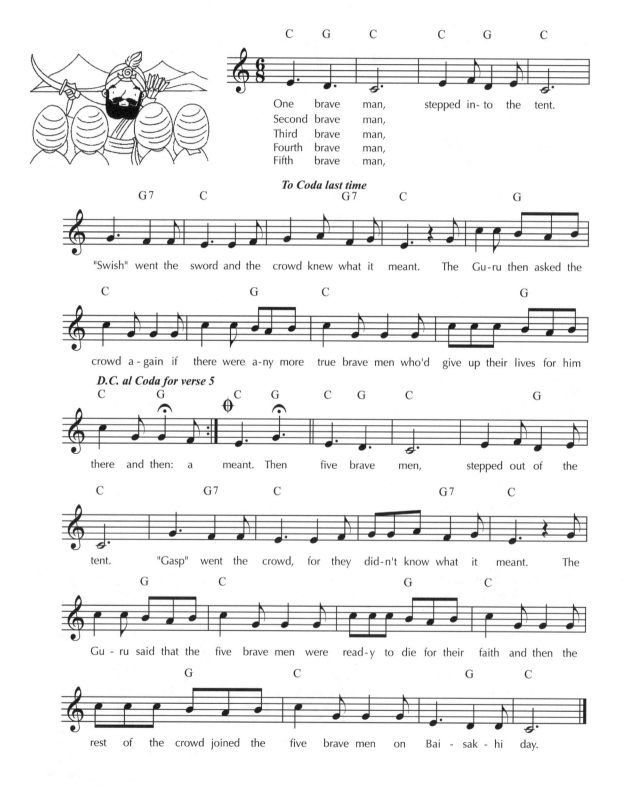

Peter Morrell

Advent calendar song

This song is sung each morning during December when the next Advent calendar window is opened.

Count - down   to   Christ - mas,   Ad - vent   is   here.

O - pen   a   win - dow   and   see   what   a - ppears.

Is   it   an   an - gel,   stock - ing   or   tree?   So

o - pen   a   win - dow,   what   do   you   see?

Sue Nicholls

Five Easter eggs

Five Eas- ter eggs in the   cor - ner ___ shop,   Wrapped in sil - ver with a   bow on ___ top.

Please can I have one   just for me!   Yes, here's one for af - ter   tea.

2. Four Easter eggs ...
3. Three Easter eggs ...
4. Two Easter eggs ...
5. One Easter egg ...

Jean Gilbert

On Good Friday

Chorus

On Good Fri - day Christ-ians say, On Good Fri - day Christ-ians say.
Eas - ter Sun - day Christ-ians say, On Eas - ter Sun - day Christ-ians say. On

On Good Fri - day Christ-ians say, Je - sus died for ev - ry one. On
Eas - ter Sun - day Christ-ians say, Je - sus came a

Slower

- live a - gain. 1.Je - sus - 's friends wept when he died.

Now they re - joice, they say He's a - live!

2. Christians are sad because he died,
   Now they rejoice they say He's alive!

John Hardwick

Ready for harvest

1. We're read - y for the har-vest. Now har-vest time has come. If
2. read - y for the har-vest. It's har-vest time a - gain. If
3. read - y for the har-vest. And now the har-vest's in. The

we're to have a har-vest, we've got to have the sun. (2.)We're
we're to have a har-vest, we've got to have the rain. (3.)We're
shar - ing of the har-vest is read - y to be - - gin.

Clive Barnwell

Janmashtami

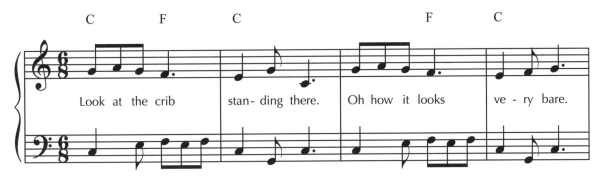

Look at the crib | stan- ding there. | Oh how it looks | ve - ry bare.

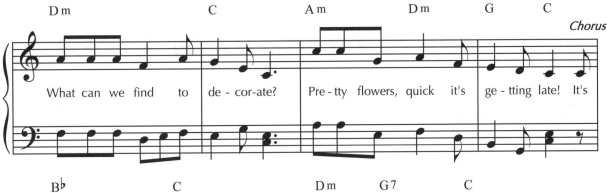

What can we find   to de - cor-ate? | Pre-tty flowers, quick it's | ge - tting late! It's

Chorus

mid - night it's ve - ry late, But | now it's ti - me to | ce - le-brate. To -

day is su-ch a | spe - cial day, For | it is Krish - na's | Bir - th day!

Look at the crib standing there,
Oh how it looks very bare.
What can we find to decorate?
Coloured sweets, quick it's getting late!

Repeat above twice and change last line
Bright tinsel, quick it's getting late!
Gold glitter, quick it's getting late!

Sally Scott

Ethiopian New Year

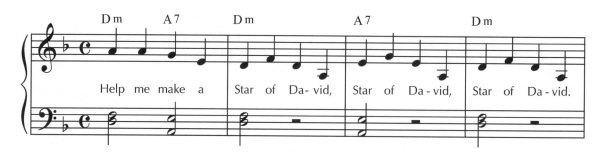

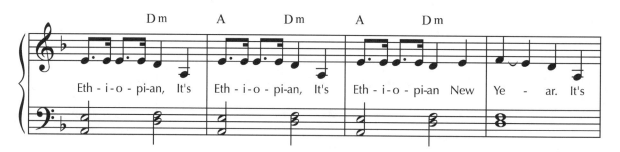

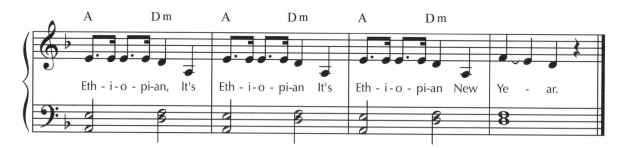

Sprinkle it with red glitter, red glitter, red glitter,
Sprinkle it with red glitter.
It's Ethiopian New Year!

Chorus

Sprinkle it with green glitter, green glitter, green glitter,
Sprinkle it with green glitter.
It's Ethiopian New Year!

Chorus

Sprinkle it with gold glitter, gold glitter, gold glitter,
Sprinkle it with gold glitter.
It's Ethiopian New Year!

Chorus

Now we've made a Star of David, Star of David,
Star of David.
Now we've made a Star of David.
It's Ethiopian New Year!

Sally Scott

Palm, myrtle, willow

Palm, myrtle, willow
Are branches children hold
To remind them of the Sukkot
Which were built in days of old.

In their other hand a citron
To remind them of their heart
As they walk around the synagogue
With each one taking part.

They also build a sukkah
Where they can eat and rest
To remind them of the forty years
Spent in the wilderness.

Brenda Williams

Long ago in Egypt

Long ago in Egypt
Moses led the way
To find a place of safety
A land where they could stay.

This was a time for packing
To follow Moses' lead.
They only took the few things
They knew that they would need.

So now as we remember,
I wonder what we'd do
If we too had to hurry off,
What would you take with you?

Brenda Williams

The Maypole rhyme

Chorus
Dancing round the Maypole,
Dancing in a ring.
Dancing round the Maypole
to welcome in the Spring.

Take your ribbon, hold it tight.
Dance with feet so neat and light.
Make your pattern round and round,
dancing on the fresh green ground.

Chorus

Keep your ribbon in your hand.
Sometimes dance and sometimes stand,
weaving neatly out and in
to help the greenwood's growth begin.

Chorus

Maypole, standing tall and lean,
brightly on our village green.
We stamp our feet and shout 'Hurray!'
to wake the spirit of the May.
*(this line can be replaced with: to
waken up the First of May!)*

Chorus

Tony Mitton

The harvest

Plums, pears and pumpkins
Ripened in the sun
Collect them for the harvest
Each and every one.

Carrots, onions, turnips
Growing all around
Dig them for the harvest
Pull them from the ground.

Oats, wheat and barley
Wavy seas of gold
Cut them for the harvest
Before the days grow cold.

Brenda Williams

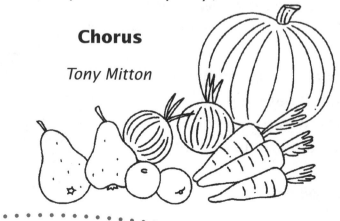

Carnival for Mardi Gras

(A steel band recording will add to the rhythm and atmosphere)

Everyone:
We're going to dance in the carnival,
for Mardi Gras.

1st Child:
I shall be a peacock and
spread my tail out wide.
Looking like a rainbow,
Twirling like a top,
and I'm never, never, never
never, NEVER going to stop!

Chorus:
(chanted by whole group, to steel band music)
We'll dance in the morning,
and we'll dance in the night,
and we'll dance through the darkness
until it is light.

2nd Child:
I shall be a butterfly,
with wings of white and yellow.
Looking like a rainbow,
Twirling like a top,
and I'm never, never, never
never, NEVER going to stop!

Chorus: (as before)

3rd Child:
I shall be a bumblebee,
dressed in gold and black.
Looking like a rainbow,
Twirling like a top,
and I'm never, never, never
never, NEVER going to stop!

Chorus: (as before)

4th Child:
I shall be a parrot,
with wings of blue and red.
Looking like a rainbow,
Twirling like a top,
and I'm never, never, never
never, NEVER going to stop!

Chorus: (as before)

5th Child:
I shall be a hummingbird,
darting to and fro.
Looking like a rainbow,
Twirling like a top,
and I'm never, never, never
never, NEVER going to stop!

Chorus: (as before)

6th Child:
I'm a bird of Paradise.
See the feathers in my tail.
Looking like a rainbow,
Twirling like a top,
and I'm never, never, never
never, NEVER going to stop!

Chorus (as before)

Other colourful characters
can be added in the same style.

Jan Pollard

Eid is coming

Eid is coming,
It's coming soon.
Ramadan ends
with the rise of the moon.

'There it is, there it is!'
we shriek and cry,
as the new moon appears
in the evening sky.

And now Eid begins
as Ramadan is past.
The feasting begins
with the end of the fast.

Tony Mitton

Holi

It is Holi. Winter is over.
We welcome the Spring.
Out in the street
with my cheerful family
I dance and sing.

We light a bonfire
to burn up rubbish and wrong.
'Good burns evil
as Spring burns Winter' –
that is the fire's song.

Rich and poor together,
from palace, from hut,
come to the fire,
Crackle the barley
and roast the nut.

This is our Springtime party
of beautiful flowers.
We scatter the colourful powder.
We sprinkle bright showers.

Come with your liveliest colours
into the street,
and sprinkle with friendship and
brightness
all that you meet.

Tony Mitton

Buddha Day

It's Buddha Day! It's Buddha Day!
See the full moon shine!
We've hung the walls with streamers
And put flowers round the shrine.

We've visited the temple
On this our holy day,
Remembering his birth and death
And how he found the way.

It's Buddha Day! It's Buddha Day!
Tonight we're staying up late
To have a family party,
To dance and celebrate.

John Foster

Festivals

Divali starts today

Putting oil lamps round the door,
Making patterns on the floor,
Sending cards to all our friends,
Happy that the monsoon ends.

Giving fruit and sticky sweets,
Lighting fireworks in the streets.
In the temple we all pray,
Now Divali starts today!

Wendy Larmont

The Rakhi

You're my little sister,
I am your big brother.
Tie a rakhi round my wrist
To bind us both together.

Thank you for the rakhi.
I am proud to wear it
And I'll leave it on for school
So my friends can admire it!

Sue Cowling

This special day

Christmas cards say many things
About this advent time
They tell of love and friendship
And the welcome, church bells chime.

They tell of our traditions
From many far off lands
How festivals around the world
Help us to join our hands

And celebrate together
In our many different ways
The birth of baby Jesus
On this special day, of days.

Brenda Williams

Chinese Lion Dance

Moving along with many feet
the lion dances up the street.
Humping his back and shaking his head,
opening his mouth, with tongue of red,
moving fowards, writhing, turning,
enormous eyes, gleaming, burning,
as the rhythm drives him on
until the lion dance is done.

Jan Pollard

Rhythm
use drums, bells and shakers as the lion dances.

Actions
Children form a long line, making the body of the lion, holding onto the waist of the child in front with their heads down. Starting off on the same foot and moving in rhythm to the music, the line should twist and turn as the children follow the movements of the leader. The child in front should wear a Chinese Lion mask. (The Chinese Lion looks the same as the Chinese Dragon.)

Guru Nanak's birthday

Today is very special.
It's full moon day, today.
We're going to the temple
To worship and to pray.

We'll listen to the stories
And share the festive food.
Everyone's excited
And in a happy mood.

Today is very special.
It's full moon day, today.
Today we're celebrating
Guru Nanak's Birthday.

John Foster

The dragon boats

The dragon boats are coming!
Listen to the gongs!
Flags are waving,
rowers splashing;
din of drumming dongs.
Red and gold the dragon heads,
jerking, racing near.
Snaky thin the dragon bodies,
straight as any spear.
Eager rowers, straining, heaving.
Fiery dragon faces.
We remember trying
to save Qu Yuan
with thrilling Dragon Boat Races!

Penny Kent

Children's Day

At school today we're celebrating
Kenji's special day.
(Children's Day in Japan
is every 5th of May.)
Gaily coloured carp streamers
hang up in the hall –
a big fish, medium, little
and a rainbow waterfall.
Kenji's mum looks lovely,
her kimono is so bright.
She showed us how to put it on
and make it look just right.
We've folded paper flowers
and an origami box.
We've seen how Kenji's best shoes
must be worn with special socks!
We're going to taste some rice-balls
and crispy crackers, too.
I'd like to do this
every year with Kenji, wouldn't you?

Penny Kent

The egg song

Peck, peck, peck,
went the little chick's beak.
Out poked its head
as it took a little peek.

Out stepped its leg.
Out flapped its wing.
Then a fluffy yellow chick
began to sing:

'Take me to the water.
Show me to the seed.
If I'm going to live and grow,
That's what I'll need!

Then when I'm a chicken,
feathery and grown,
I can cluck and lay an egg
all of my own!'

Tony Mitton

Baisakhi days

Some wear a football strip with pride,
And stand with team-mates at their side.

Some wear uniforms of their groups.
Of Brownies, Beavers, Rainbow troops.

Some wear the colours of their school
On jumpers, jerseys, fleece, cagoule.

Some wave a flag, or sing a song.
So many things show we belong.

Sikhs all celebrate Baisakhi days
And remember then, the first 5Ks.

Brenda Williams

Let's celebrate!

Let's celebrate St David's day
And wear a daffodil
To show that we remember him
And think about him still.

Let's celebrate St Patrick's day
With a shamrock of bright green.
We'll wear it pinned upon our coats
To let three leaves be seen.

Let's celebrate St George's day
With a bright red rose to wear.
For he was brave and fearless
Where others would not dare.

Let's celebrate St Andrew's day
With a thistle or with heather
And dance a Scottish highland fling
Around the room together!

Brenda Williams

 # A story for Holi

Once, long ago, a king lived in India. His name was Hiranyakashup. He was so proud and rich and powerful that he thought that he could do anything he wanted. He had a little boy called Prahlada. Hiranyakashup told Prahlada that he was God. So Prahlada thought that his father Hiranyakashup was God, and every day, when he said his prayers, he prayed to his own father, and not to God.

Prahlada grew up into a young man. He still believed that his father was God. Then, one day, Prahlada was out walking in the town near his father's palace, when he heard a potter praying out loud. The potter was very upset. "What's the matter?" Prahlada asked. The potter said, "I put some big pots into the hot oven to bake hard, and I didn't know that a mother cat had just put all her kittens into the biggest pot. They will all be burned in the hot oven. I'm praying to Lord Vishnu* to save the kittens." Prahlada was puzzled. "Who is Lord Vishnu? Why are you not praying to Hiranyakashup? He is our god and king." The potter said, "Lord Vishnu is the king of all kings, and he is God, not Hiranyakashup. The king is only a man." The potter took his big pots out of the oven. Prahlada heard a little sound, "Miaow, miaow, miaow." The kittens were alive! God had heard the potter's prayer, and saved them.

From that day, Prahlada knew that Hiranyakashup was not God. He would not bow down to him and pray to him any more. Hiranyakashup was very angry with him. Soon he began to hate Prahlada, and he tried to kill him. First he put Prahlada into a pit full of snakes. Prahlada prayed to God to save him. The snakes crawled all over Prahlada, but they didn't bite him. He was saved by God. Then one night Prahlada was asleep on the ground, and the wicked king sent his elephants to trample all over Prahlada. The elephants walked carefully all round Prahlada. Again he was saved by God. Hiranyakashup sent his soldiers to kill Prahlada with their swords. But when the soldiers tried to kill him, their swords were turned aside. Once more he was saved by God.

Hiranyakashup was angrier than ever. He went to his sister Holika. "Help me to get rid of Prahlada, Holika," said the king. Holika had a magic gift from God. Fire couldn't burn her. She said, "Build a bonfire, and I will ask Prahlada to climb up to the top of it with me. Tell the soldiers to set fire to the bonfire. I will be safe, but Prahlada will be burnt to death in the fire." Prahlada climbed to the top of the huge bonfire with her, and the soldiers set fire to it. But God was watching. He broke Holika's magic, and once again he saved Prahlada. So Holika was the one who was burnt in the fire.

Now, every year at Holi, people light a bonfire to remember the story of Prahlada and Holika, and how good overcame evil.

* Vishnu is the name Hindu people call God.

Barbara Moore

The story of Baisakhi

Balbir was in Mrs Johnson's class. One day, Mr Singh, her daddy, came to tell them about a festival called Baisakhi. He showed the children a picture. "This is Guru Nanak," he said. "What kind of man do you think he was?" The children looked at the picture. Guru Nanak was old. He was wearing a white robe and had a white turban on his head. He had a long white beard. There was a ring of light round his head.

John said, "He looks like Father Christmas." Mr Singh laughed. "Yes, he does a bit." Anna said, "He looks like a holy man who prays to God a lot." Mr Singh nodded. "He was a very holy man. His name was Nanak, and he was the first guru – 'Guru' means teacher. He started the Sikh religion. Now look at this picture. This is the last guru – Guru Gobind Singh. What kind of man was he, do you think?" The children looked. This picture was different. Guru Gobind Singh was young. He had a black beard and a bright coloured turban. He was riding a horse. He had a fierce-looking bird on his wrist and a sword by his side. "He looks like a soldier," Paul said. Mr Singh agreed. "That's right. He had to fight. That's where the story of Baisakhi begins...

One day, a long time ago, thousands of Sikhs came to meet Guru Gobind Singh. It was New Year's Day – Baisakhi. Everyone was very worried, because people were attacking Sikhs and killing them. When the Guru came out of his tent, he was dressed in a yellow tunic, with a blue sash round the middle. He wore a turban on his head and carried a long sword in his hand. The crowd waited to hear what the Guru would say.

'Who is ready to give up everything for God?' he shouted. 'Who will give me his head?' Everyone was shocked. Nobody said a word. At last, one man stepped forward. He was a shopkeeper. 'I am not afraid to die for God,' he said. The Guru took him into the tent. Everything was very quiet. There was a thud. When the Guru

came out of the tent his sword was red with blood. 'Who else will give up his head?' he asked. Nobody spoke. Then another man stepped forward. He was a farmer. He said, 'I am ready to die for God,' and he went into the tent with the Guru. Again, there was a thud, and the Guru came out of the tent with blood dripping from his sword. People stared in horror. Three more times the Guru asked, 'Who else will die for God?' One by one a washerman, a barber and a water-carrier came forward and followed the Guru into the tent. Everyone believed the Guru had chopped off the heads of the five brave men with his sword.

But then, out of the tent came the Guru – with all the five men behind him. The crowd gasped in amazement. They were not dead after all – they were alive. They were dressed like the Guru, in yellow tunics with blue sashes, and they wore turbans on their heads. The Guru said, 'These men were ready to give their lives for God. Now they

wear a turban?" Mr Singh said, "Well, after Guru Gobind Singh chose the Five Beloved at Baisakhi, he gave the Sikhs a sort of uniform. My turban is part of the uniform, and so is this bracelet I'm wearing on my wrist." Mr Singh had brought a turban with him. The children were surprised to see how long it was. When Mr Singh held one end and John held the other, it reached right across the classroom. Mr Singh wound the turban round John's head, to show the children how to do it.

Then it was playtime. The children liked the story so much that they asked Mrs Johnson if they could do an assembly about it when Baisakhi

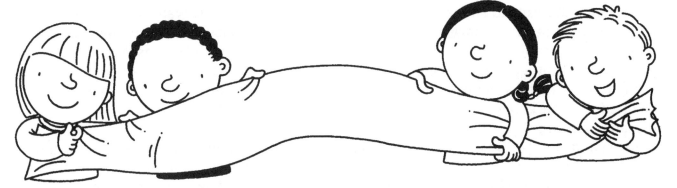

are the Five Beloved – holy men, and soldiers. They are the first members of the new brotherhood of Sikhs.'"

Mr Singh looked at the children. "That's the story of Baisakhi," he said. "Every year, Sikhs all over the world have a festival, and remember that story."

Mrs Johnson stood up. "What an exciting story, Mr Singh. Thank you for telling us it. Now, does anyone want to ask Mr Singh any questions?" Balbir's friend Katie put up her hand. "Mr Singh, why did the Guru and the men wear turbans? And why do you

came. Mrs Johnson said, "Yes, but I'll have to read the bit where the guru asks if anyone will give up his life for God, because Sikhs don't usually like anyone to pretend to be the Guru." They practised acting the story, and everyone came to the Baisakhi assembly. Balbir's mummy and daddy both came, and they clapped longest of all.

Barbara Moore

The story of Divali Festival of Lights

Divali is a joyful festival celebrated by both Hindus and Sikhs. The Hindu version celebrates the story of Rama and Sita, and their return to their home after fourteen years of exile in the jungles.

Rama was a prince. He had a favourite brother called Lakshman whom he loved very much. They were good friends and loved to go hunting together with their golden bows and arrows.

Now a king from another part of the country was looking for a husband for his beautiful daughter Sita. He had a special, heavy bow which was very hard to bend, so he sent a message to all the princes that whoever could bend this great bow would be able to marry Sita.

Many princes tried, but no one else could even lift it! When it was Rama's turn, however, he lifted the bow easily and bent it so much it snapped in two.

Rama and Sita were married. The old king wanted Rama to be the next king, but the queen would not hear of it. She wanted her own son to rule. Because the king loved his wife and wanted to please her, he arranged for Rama and Sita to be sent far away, to live in a land of thick jungle. Lakshman went with them.

The three of them lived simply and happily in their jungle home for many years. But far away a wicked demon with ten heads, called Ravana, heard about Sita's beauty and wanted to steal her from Rama. He tricked Sita away from the safety of her home and took her to his palace.

Rama and Lakshman searched for Sita for many days and nights. Then Hanuman, a monkey god, offered to help them. He could travel very fast, over the treetops, and saw Sita in the garden of Ravana's palace. Hanuman gave Sita a ring from Rama and told her she would soon be rescued.

With the monkeys of Hanuman's army beside them, Rama and Lakshman fought a long and terrible battle with Ravana and his demons. The monkeys made a bridge of stones so that the two princes could reach the demon's island. Finally, Rama took a magic arrow – given to him by the sun god, Indira – and shot it straight into Ravana's wicked heart. At last the monster was killed.

It was time for Rama to return home with Sita.

While Rama had been away his father had died, so the people were very happy when the young prince returned to them. He was crowned King with Sita beside him.

All the streets were decorated, there were beautiful fireworks and every house was lit with tiny lamps, making the whole city look like a fairyland.

All this happened a long, long time ago. Today, Hindus celebrate the festival of Divali every winter. They light their homes with little pottery lamps – called diva – and fairy lights. They have special food and new clothes and give each other gifts. It is a very happy occasion.

Pronunciation guide	
Sita	*See-tah*
Lakshman	*Luksh-mun*
Ravana	*Rah-vun*
Hanuman	*Han-u-mahn*
Diva	*Thee-yah*
Divali	*Thee-vah-lee*

Susheila Stone

(Abridged from the original)

The Chinese New Year story

There were only a few days to New Year and twelve of the animals were arguing. Each animal wanted the new year named after himself. What a noise they made! Roaring, crowing, bleating, hissing, barking and squeaking. They soon woke the gods who appeared in the sky and asked what was going on. All the animals answered at once.

"Be quiet!" ordered the gods. "You are all very rude!"

The animals went quiet. One by one they explained why they were arguing and why each felt the new year should be named after them.

The gods listened to them and thought very hard about their problem. They finally decided it would be best to hold a race.

"Can you see the big river?" the gods asked. 'You must all swim across it, and we will name the new year after the one who reaches the other side first.'

The animals all agreed to take part. Secretly, each thought they would win. They lined up along the bank and the gods started them off.

"Ready, steady GO!" they shouted.

There was an enourmous splash as the twelve animals leaped into the water. Ox was the strongest swimmer and he soon began to take the lead. When Rat saw this, he cleverly grabbed Ox's tail and climbed onto his back without Ox noticing. As Ox waded the last few steps to the bank, Rat leaped over his head and onto the shore.

"I've won! I've won!" he squeaked.

Ox was very surprised. He had no idea that Rat had cheated.

So the gods named the new year after Rat. "Next year will be the year of the Ox because he was second," they said.

One by one the other animals reached the other side of the river, Tiger, Hare, Dragon, Snake, Horse, Ram, Monkey, Cockerel, Dog and then Pig, who came last.

"You have all done very well," said the gods, "so we will name a year after each one of you, in the same order that you finished the race."

The animals were very tired, but pleased that it was all settled and they didn't have to argue any more!

Jackie Andrews